A Dusty Garden GROWS

BY TERRY CLOTHIER THOMPSON

A Dusty Garden Grows

Author: Terry Clothier Thompson

Editor: Edie McGinnis
Technical Editor: Deb McCurnin
Designer: Amy Robertson
Photography: Aaron T. Leimkuehler
Illustration: Lon Eric Craven
Production assistance by Jo Ann Groves

Published by:
Kansas City Star Books
1729 Grand Blvd.
Kansas City, Missouri, USA 64108

First edition, first printing
978-1-933466-66-8

Library of Congress Control Number: 2008930244

Printed in the United States of America
by Walsworth Publishing Co., Marceline, MO

To order copies, call StarInfo at (816) 234-4636 and say "Books."

Table of Contents

ABOUT THE AUTHOR
Terry Clothier Thompson

Terry Clothier Thompson has been on the forefront of our current quilt revival.

Born into the fifth generation of a Kansas pioneer family, she grew up in the Wichita area. She watched her grandmother sew and quilt during visits to the family farm called Peace Creek, west of Hutchinson, Kansas.

Her stitching passion began when she sewed calico dresses for her daughter.

With the leftover scraps, she made a quilt and, in the process, became a passionate quilter.

Her family's move to Kansas City brought the opportunity to teach patchwork at Johnson County Community College. In 1973, she opened "The Quilting Bee," a store devoted totally to quilting, an anomaly at that time. The shop was located on the Country Club Plaza until 1984. She designed a unique line of patterns that she still sells nationwide. Terry was a principal documenter for the Kansas Quilt Project from 1986 to 1989 and was a co-author of Kansas Quilts and Quilters, published in 1993 by the University Press of Kansas.

In addition to her appliqué patterns, Terry has written six books through her company, Peace Creek Patterns and Books. Each is a collection of family stories in different eras and has quilts designed to go along with the stories. She has published the following books with the Kansas City Star, "Four Block Quilts," "Libertyville," "Quilts in Red and Green," and "Red, Green, and Beyond" with Nancy Hornback, "Quilts Through the Camera's Eye," and "Louisa May Alcott."

Her passion for quiltmaking is contagious. She has an extensive collection of vintage fabrics, quilts, laces and all kinds of needlework. Terry's FabriCamp© classes are held in her new studio in Lawrence, Kansas. She also designs a line of reproduction fabrics for Moda. For more information about Terry, check out her web site: terrythompson.com.

She raised two children and enjoys her four wonderful grandchildren.

Acknowledgements

Thanks to Jean Stanclift, Karalee Fisher, Pam Mayfield, Eula Lang, Nan Doljac, Lori Kukuk, and Nancy Hornback. I appreciate all the help they gave me with the appliqué work, piecing, quilting and binding. I especially want to thank Nancy for lending me her Sunbonnet Sue quilt. Thanks and gratitude to Rosie Mayhew for her Pansy design and the Kansas Capital Quilt Guild for the Pansy quilt blocks given to me after a fire destroyed my home in 1997.

Thanks to Sarah Stanclift for the clerical and computer work and Jack Webb for his help with props and computer work.

I appreciate all the encouragement I received from the people at Quilting Bits and Pieces in Eudora, Kansas, and for their help with ordering fabric.

Thanks go to Aaron Leimkuhler for his lovely photos, to Amy Robertson for her eye-catching page design, Lon Eric Craven for his wonderful illustrations, Jo Ann Groves for her imaging skills, Diane McLendon, marketing manager, Edie McGinnis, my editor, and Doug Weaver, my publisher.

Foreword

Providing electricity to rural America became a big issue for Congress and for Franklin D. Roosevelt's administration. After many pro and con debates and much discussion on how to finance such a large effort to electrify American farms, the Rural Electrification Administration was formed by Roosevelt on May 11, 1935. Initially the REA was viewed as a relief agency, and according to the *The Next Greatest Thing* (see bibliography) one year later, May 21, 1936, Congress approved a bill giving the REA regular appropriations and full status as a government agency.

A new world opened for America's farm families, who now had the electric power to light the night. Children no longer huddled around kerosene lamps at the table to do their homework. Electric motors provided power for farm machinery and tools.

For housewives, the drudgery of washing clothes on a washboard in a tub, churning butter by hand, ironing with a 6 or 7 pound iron, and cooking on a woodstove became a thing of the past. People were able to read, sew and mend at night without having their eyesight harmed.

Later surveys would find that the educational level of rural children had improved markedly with the introduction of electricity. Water could now be pumped into the house for bathing and cooking rather than being hauled in one bucket at a time. The lady of the house could choose when to can the fresh produce she brought in from her garden since the refrigerator would keep it fresh for a few days. Indoor plumbing was probably the most appreciated convenience.

To learn more about the efforts to light up rural America and know how it impacted lives, read *The Next Greatest Thing–50 years of Rural Electrification in America.* 1 -1984- NRECA.

1900-1939

DIARY OF ANNA ELIZABETH MARSHALL CLOTHIER

BASED ON TERRY'S FAMILY STORIES AND RECOLLECTIONS

WRITTEN BY TERRY CLOTHIER THOMPSON

My life on the prairie — the beauty of the tall waving grass, the brilliant sunsets of pink, orange and blue and the sunrises of blended colors of red, purple and orange. The grass is green. The sky is blue — my eyes search everywhere for signs of colors, and today the first spring wildflowers caught my eye as if they had been there all along, just waiting for me to discover their beauty. I have learned to see God's earthly gifts in a different way than before when I took nature's bounty for granted. In Kentucky, where I was born, I was surrounded by so many trees and gardens of flowers, that I grew spoiled and never appreciated their shapes and colors. I never really "looked" at flowers; I only saw them as a mass of colors. Now, here at Peace Creek, my hungry eyes search for any sign of colors other than the green of grass, the blue of sky, the dull tan of sandy soil.

Pieced quilts are on every bed. I started piecing quilts at the age of five when Mother showed me how to sew four square patches of calico into rows, then sew those rows together to form the simple four-patch quilt block. I mastered the four-patch block very quickly and then I started piecing nine-patch blocks which had nine calico patches and a more interesting design to it

When I was eight years old, I pieced my first Evening Star quilt blocks. The pieces were much smaller than a nine patch square and this was the

Mail order seeds arrived today just as I finished turning over the garden bed. The soil is so light and sandy, it hardly seems like work to prepare the ground for seeding. I ordered my seeds from that new catalogue I saw at the Peace Creek general store, Burpee, who guarantees their seeds will germinate. I will plant by the moon signs according to the almanac, to be assured of a fruitful crop of vegetables and a beautiful flowering palette of new colors surrounding our home. The bulbs, given to me by my friends and family, were planted last fall and are showing tiny green leaves peeking through the soil for the first time.

Coxcomb, carnations, tulips, love apples, or tomatoes as my new neighbors call them, seem to flourish in the good soil and sunshine here at Peace Creek. When we left Missouri, I placed some rooted roses inside a cored potato. The potato kept the roots moist and ready to plant when we arrived at our homestead acres in Kansas. Roses grow exceptionally well, as long as I keep the gophers at bay. It is our good fortune that some good nurseryman planted oak trees for shade, and cottonwood trees are native to Kansas and grow in generous supply around our farmstead.

I just gave birth to a new baby girl. My brood of youngsters now numbers 15. Now that the older ones are of the age to help out more with the little ones, my determination is to make my first appliquéd quilt. Now, I piece my quilts in my spare moments at nap time and evening before bed. Kansas winters are cold and harsh, so I must supply our own warm bedding. I do love to make quilts. Not only are they important to our well-being, they satisfy the part of me that craves beauty and order in this hard, plain life. To tuck my children in under three or four quilts that come from my own hand and mind swells my heart with joy. I believe I inherited the talent for using the needle from Mother and Grandmother.

first time I ever pieced triangles into a quilt block. It offered a nice break from just piecing squares. I wanted my blocks to be pieced with a consistent color combination on each block, which meant that I had to piece very small scraps or strips of cloth together to create just one small square or triangle. I still have those Evening Star quilt blocks from my girlhood, sitting in a neat stack in my travel trunk.

Someday I will have the time to set the blocks together for a small quilt for one of the children. Or maybe a daughter or granddaughter will finish them into a quilt for her children. I think it is all right for one generation of women to finish quilts the older generation was just too busy or tired to complete. We all help each other out in this country. We need everyone's helping hand, now and then, to make life not so hard and wearisome.

Resurrection Plant

This brief time reminded me of the resurrection plant, a, fern-like cluster of gray-green leaves that curled into a ball of dried, brownish, dead-looking matter. When watered, though, it opened and greened in a short time, a miracle to me.

—Patricia Wilson Clothier

At night, I see the eerie glow of smoke and prairie fires off to the Northwest up around the salt marsh. As long as the wind is from the south, our home and fields will be safe. I pray for rain day and night, as every stem of grass and tree is tinder dry from these last two years of drought. The hot winds fan the flames that can destroy a homestead and a year's farm work in a matter of minutes. Peace Creek has not run dry yet, but if we don't get rain soon, we will have to haul water for our cattle and horses.

One of the most destructive plagues is upon us. Because of the drought, grasshoppers have multiplied into thousands of insatiable eating insects. Nothing escapes their jaws — crops and fields are devastated, my garden has been stripped, my beautiful flowers are gone. The girls and I fight their entry into the house, hoping there will be relief soon from this menace. We hung the wash out on the line; they even ate the green stripes out of Gertie's cotton dress. We fondly remember that dress from the small scraps sewn into the Lemon Star quilt she pieced last winter.

New owners of the Peace Creek store have moved into the living quarters behind the store. They are from back east and are said to be well connected with merchants and shippers who will keep us well supplied with calico, needles and thread for our dresses and cotton batting for our quilts. Goods will be coming more on trains now, rather than overland by wagons.

Peace Creek now has a post office, a creamery, a blacksmith and the most wonderful general store in these parts. C.E. Miller and his wife, Sarah, have brought commerce and supplies to us beyond our expectations. We only have to travel a mile by horse or

The Low Point

The window framed difficult times for all living creatures in the hills and across the plains below. If the economy didn't affect lives, the stark and bitter drought wrought trouble for the people and other living things.
—PATRICIA WILSON CLOTHIER

wagon to get there and we have to remind the boys of chores to be done before they are to meet their friends at the store.

Dust storms have come to Peace Creek. We suffer with drought and the price of wheat dropped so low folks are selling their wheat at prices lower than it cost to produce. Everyone feels the hard times upon us. The small creeks and ponds have dried up so we

haul water for the livestock from our well and save some for washing clothes. We are blessed that our well has not gone dry.

The dust is so bad that daylight looks like late evening. Babies spit up dust they have breathed, there is little left of the white paint on our home. After leaving church services this Sunday, the Keesling family had to walk the four miles from church to their homestead. The dust became worse and they could not see to walk without falling off the road into the ditch. Irlene said they saw a bright light moving slowly in front of them that led them home safely. They never knew who or what provided the light that showed them the way home.

We here at Peace Creek are seeing better times, thanks to the government programs that have helped get people back on their feet. Electricity has finally come to the rural areas of Kansas. Today my girls and I rejoiced at the sight of the linemen who came today to hook us up to electricity and phone service! My husband ordered an electric stove and refrigerator. Soon the indoor plumbing will be in operation. Most cities have had electricity since the 1890's, why has it taken so long for country folks to have the same convenience?

The time has finally come to begin my first appliquéd quilt. A great deal of thought goes into the making of my quilts and I have been supplied with many patterns and ideas from Mrs. S. over the years. And I have my own ideas as well. Although my work load has been eased, most of my time is taken up by the children, neighbors and the work of the church.

So I have decided to try my ideas for lessening the time it takes to make an appliquéd quilt.

Instead of making twelve or more smaller blocks, I want to make four large blocks, each measuring 36" square. I will add borders to frame the four blocks, just like the picture that hangs in the hallway. I found I could make the appliqué patterns larger by tracing circles around my dinner plate for large flowers and roses and use a saucer or teacup for smaller, layered flowers. The ends of a spool of thread serve nicely for a pattern for berries, since the flowers must be exaggerated in size. Also, by folding muslin or paper in half, I only have to draw half of the shape. When I cut it out, the shape is the same on both sides.

Today my husband is hitching old Trelby to the two-seated buggy and driving me to the Peace Creek General Store to buy my cotton fabrics for my appliqué quilt. There will be no matching of scraps in this quilt. I have saved enough of my egg money to buy bleached white cotton muslin for my blocks and borders and enough red, pink, green and yellow for the appliqués.

Cactus and Grass

The quest was the thing. We gloried in the feather from a white-winged dove, treasured a rock that sparkled, collected a twisted length of bleached mesquite, or found an unusual cactus in bloom.

— PATRICIA WILSON CLOTHIER

Mrs. Miller orders fabric from the salesman's sample cards, cottons that she thinks the women here in Peace Creek will enjoy wearing and putting into their quilts. She cannot possibly order everything that is available, but I think she does well buying such a variety of designs. Many of the cotton prints have odd but interesting shapes such as interlocking circles, rectangles or triangles with a choice of different background colors such as white, blue, red or brown.

Winter on the prairie provides the best time to start the appliqué quilt I have been planning. I chose the Coxcomb and Currant pattern and enlarged it to fit the four 36" square blocks of bleached muslin that I have cut, ironed and folded.

Wednesday mornings at the Peace Creek Church, the older women of the congregation hold a Ladies Bible Teaching class for all the younger women and girls. After class we all eat our basket dinners together in the church basement where tables and chairs have been set up. I so look forward to Wednesdays as a day of fellowship with my friends and neighbors. We share recipes and news in the community and it is a time that we seem to be able to express our ideas and viewpoints freely, away from the critical ears of our husbands and fathers.

After we break bread together, we women who are quilt makers in the group set up the quilting frames and quilt each other's quilt tops. The younger children play or nap underneath the quilt canopy and the older children help keep the needles threaded and listen to their mother's conversation.

I have planned a surprise for our next quilting bee at church. Several quilting friends who enjoy appliqué have expressed their interest in my appliqué patterns. Like me, they don't have the time to make 20 or 25 small blocks but can manage four large ones. Ideas for patterns are nearly bursting from my head and I long to share them. I have packed the buggy with my drawings and patterns along with two freshly baked sandhill plum pies to take to the Wednesday meeting. I mustn't forget to take the paper and a pencil for tracing.

Century Plant

A prickly-pear cactus edged the wall near the old fig tree. June bugs tasted the sticky fruits. Nearby, the maguey or century plant grew waiting to send out its one stalk with plants of yellow flower clusters from the blue-gray, agave base.

—Patricia Wilson Clothier

Many piecers were converted today when they began to see how much fun it is to make a "flower quilt" that is so different from the everyday pieced scrap quilts. Quilt friends look to me for guidance as I have made many quilts, especially the young married girls who are just starting their own homes and want their quilts to look different from their mother's bedding.

Seventeen of us met on Saturday and we all went to the Peace Creek Store to do our trading. I declare, but we were excited to be in that store, laying out the bolts of calico on Mrs. Miller's cutting table! Colors of red, yellow, orange and apple green caught my fancy. There was a wide choice of double pink prints. One had red seaweed figures cleverly printed on the background. The snow-white bleached muslin was greatly admired by everyone for its quality and fine thread count. Most of us chose a combination of red, green, pink and an accent of yellow, gold or orange. Some women chose red, yellow and blue as the colors for their quilt. We all agreed to meet at my farmhouse in April to cut out the appliqués. By then the spring snows will have melted and the horse teams could pull the wagons and buggies down the rough county roads.

Seventeen enthusiastic appliquers sat around my large oak tables in the kitchen. A feeling of sisterhood drew us all together in the excitement of trying something new and different. Several women chose to work together as a team, one making the blocks, the other making the borders. Each person chose a different pattern to appliqué and no two were alike. I tried my best to give advice and instructions at the beginning of our quilt day, but it soon was out of my hands as each person or team came along with their own ideas of how they would work their own particular pattern. Many ideas and appliqué techniques were explored that day, as we all learned from each other.

My cousin Irlene came to help me serve the luncheon and declared she was leaving as soon as lunch was served. She caught the "fever" and had her Tulips blocks cut out and basted before we called a close to the day.

We had decided to make our blocks throughout the summer months and agreed to meet again at my home in October for tea to show our flowering quilt blocks to one another. We thought it would be interesting to keep track of the hours spent on one block and report the difficulty of each pattern.

Summer passed so quickly. All I recall is appliquéing my Coxcomb and Currant blocks and going into the orchard to pray for my boys' reckless ways. What have I done? Today at Sunday meeting I asked Lucy as to the whereabouts of her mother, Doris. Lucy smiled sheepishly and whispered that her mother was at home working on her Rose of Sharon appliqué blocks so she would be finished in time for our October tea!

Indian summer at Peace Creek makes one forget the hot, windy days of August and September. The ladies began arriving early in the afternoon for tea and sharing their appliquéd "gardens." My words will barely be able to describe the color and joy of the day. All had finished their blocks and many had even begun their borders. All my friends expressed their surprise and wonder at how easily and quickly they finished their big blocks. At first some doubted that they would like the red, green, pumpkin and white colors, but all loved their fabric choices after they saw their blocks finished. The comment that was expressed by everyone was that appliqué is so "forgiving" because points and corners don't have to be cut, marked and pieced so precisely as in pieced quilts.

Miss Miller has arthritis and the same numbness in her hands that I have from churning butter and kneading bread. She reported that the large appliquéd pieces were easier for her fingers to hold and sew, thus relieving her of hand cramps. I observed all levels of appliqué skill and yet every block was a beautiful work of art. Irlene had not only appliquéd her four blocks, but had her quilt top entirely quilted and finished to be admired by all at the fall tea. Doris got her share of teasing for missing church. When the sun set over the west end of the house and the east porch provided good shade, we all took our chairs outside for a photograph of all of us together with our appliquéd blocks.

Dust Bowl Days and Dust Bowl Days Are Over

I designed two quilts using thirteen unusual floral patterns by Laura Wheeler, Ruth Finley, Nancy Cabot and Sophie LaCroix, published in 1928 through 1935. The patterns are stylized renderings of flowers familiar to all who love plants and gardening. The schoolhouse and houses represent the men, women and children who lived during World War I and the Great Depression. They were the folks who fought drought, giant wind and sand storms, falling wheat prices and great inconvenience. Their lives were made harder by the lack of electricity available to rural areas.

The brown quilt tells the story of the women who lived in the Midwest and suffered through the dust storms that turned their world brown. The quotes and stories emphasize the positive attitude and cleverness women showed during times of hardship. With the help of letters and newspaper accounts written by and about women, I discovered the joy and comfort flowers brought to them. I included photographs of women posing in their gardens that convey how flowers brightened their lives.

The blue quilt, with its brighter colors, signifies the return to prosperity for rural families. It speaks of the importance of having telephones and electricity installed and how it eased the daily drudgery and made for more efficient farming and housekeeping.

DUST BOWL DAYS

Quilt Size 77" x 77"
Appliquéd by Jean Stanclift · Quilted by Nan Doljac

Dust Bowl Days

Read all instructions before beginning the quilts and projects. Refer to the template pages for cutting directions for the appliqué pieces.

YARDAGE:

✳ 5 3/4 yards of background for 13 - 14 1/2" squares, 8 side setting triangles, 4 corner triangles and the outside border. Choose fabric that looks like a dust storm with flecks of light and dark colors.

✳ 1 – 2 fat quarters each of red, green, yellow, pink, blue, brown and purple batiks for flowers and houses. Use scraps for more variety.

✳ 2 yards gold for inside border and binding.

CUTTING DIRECTIONS:

✳ 13 - 14 1/2" squares from the background fabric.

✳ 2 - 21 1/8" squares. Cut each square from corner to corner twice on the diagonal to make 8 side setting triangles - see Fig. 1 on page 53.

✳ 2 - 10 7/8" squares. Cut each square once on the diagonal to make 4 triangles. See Fig. 2 on page 53.

SEWING DIRECTIONS:

All blocks are set on point and you will find a small piecing diagram along with the template pages. Prepare all appliqué shapes for hand or machine appliqué. Some pattern pieces may be partially pieced, such as the Iris, Dogwood, Crocus, Aunt Amy's House and Wide Awake School house, then appliquéd to the background. Follow the instructions for each block. Pin and baste all appliqué shapes onto the background squares before sewing in place.

FINISHING INSTRUCTIONS:

To set the quilt together, refer to the diagram on page 53. Sew each row of blocks on the diagonal, with a setting triangle sewn to the end of each of the rows. Start with the corner triangles as shown in the diagram.

When all the blocks and triangles are sewn together, measure the quilt through the center from top to bottom. Cut and sew enough 3" gold strips together to equal that measurement for the two side borders. Measure the quilt through the center again. Sew enough 3" gold strips together to equal that measurement for the top and bottom border and sew in place. Measure the quilt through the center again. Cut enough 6 1/2" brown strips to equal that measurement for the two sides and the top and bottom border. Sew the borders in place.

QUILT AND BIND

BLOCK 1:
Dogwood

Refer to the templates on page 30 for the cutting directions for the appliqué pieces. You will find the placement diagram there as well.

Piece the A and A reversed petals into 4 large petals. Place the two C shapes along the edge of the square with the raw edges parallel to the edge of the square. Turn the inside edge of piece C under and appliqué in place. Center the 4 petals on the background square and slip piece D into the V shape at the top of each petal. Appliqué in place. Piece the B square together and appliqué over the edges of the petals in the center of the flower.

BLOCK 2:

Mariposa Lily

Refer to the templates on page 31 for the cutting directions for the appliqué pieces. You will find the placement diagram there as well.

Lay out and pin the stems and leaves on the background square. Pin the petals and calyx in place. Appliqué all pieces onto the background square.

BLOCK 3:
Calla Lily

Refer to the templates on pages 32-34 for the cutting directions for the appliqué pieces. You will find the placement diagram there as well.

Sew leaf F and F reversed together and place along the edge of the square.

Pin piece D to the background fabric as shown in the placement diagram on page 32. Next, place piece E, then group pieces B, A and C. Appliqué all to the background fabric.

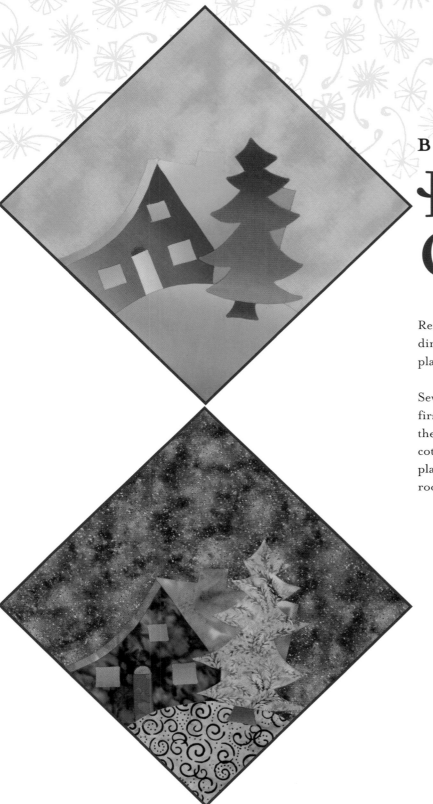

BLOCK 4:

Hillside Cottage

Refer to the templates on pages 35-36 for the cutting directions for the appliqué pieces. You will find the placement diagram there as well.

Sew windows A, B, C, door D and roof F to the cottage first. Pin piece G in place. Pin the hill to the corner of the background square, then line up the edge of the cottage against the raw edge of the square. Appliqué all in place. Pin pine tree I and trunk H over the middle of the roof and stitch in place. Refer to the photo if necessary.

BLOCK 5:

Wide Awake School House

Refer to the templates on page 37 for the cutting directions for the appliqué pieces. You will find the placement diagram there as well. There are no templates given for the following pieces.

3 - 1 1/2" x 10" strips from red fabric
3 – 1 1/2" x 10" strips from brown fabric
1 – 1" x 10" bias strip from tan fabric
1 – 11 7/8" green square. Cut the square once on the diagonal. You will have one triangle left over.

Match up the edges and corners of the green triangle with the edges of the background square. Turn the top edge of the green triangle under and appliqué to the background square. Trim the background area away from under the green triangle.

Sew the red and brown strips together alternating the colors. Pin to the background square and appliqué in place.

Pin the roof in place. Note: there is not a triangle in the roof. The 1/2" tan strip is appliquéd on to the roof and down the side of the schoolhouse and over the pieced "logs."

Stitch the roof to the log house. Then appliqué the windows in place.

Field Daisy

Refer to the templates on page 38 for the cutting directions for the appliqué pieces. You will find the placement diagram there as well.

Place the points of leaf A along the raw edge of the square and pin in place. Pin piece B to the center of piece A. Petals C and C reverse go on the left and right of the D petals. Refer to the diagram on page 38. Appliqué all pieces in place.

BLOCK 7:
Iris

Refer to the templates on pages 40-41 for the cutting directions for the appliqué pieces. You will find the placement diagram there as well.

Sew petal A and A reverse together. Then sew petal B and B reverse together. Tuck and pin the top petals into the center of the lower petals.

The C and C reversed leaves are placed against the raw edges of square with the center stem D in between the leaves.

Pin the pieced Iris blossom on top of the center stem. The large leaves should overlap the petals slightly. Appliqué all to the background square.

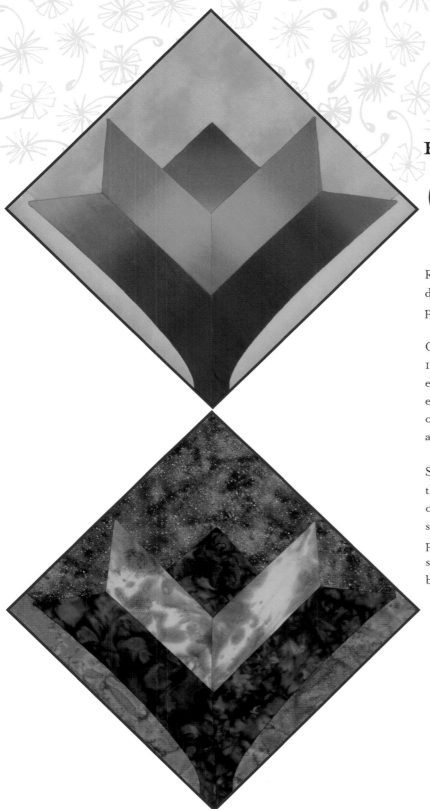

Crocus

Refer to the templates on pages 42-43 for the cutting directions for the appliqué pieces. You will find the placement diagram there as well.

Cut 2 – 1 3/4" x 13 1/2" strips of green. Press under a 1/4" seam allowance on one edge. Line up the long raw edge with the raw edge of the block. Appliqué the turned edge to the background square. (The strips will not overlap in the corner but will be covered up by other appliqué pieces.)

Stitch the C and C reversed pieces together. Stitch the B and B reversed pieces together. Pin the point of the outer C petals to the corner of the background square over the green leaves. Place the pieced B inner petals slightly under the outer petals. Tuck the A square slightly under the B petals. Appliqué all to the background square.

BLOCK 9:

Uncle Wilbur's Home

Refer to the templates on pages 44-45 for the cutting directions for the appliqué pieces. You will find the placement diagram there as well.

Cut an 11 7/8" square from brown/green fabric. Cut once on the diagonal to make triangles (see figure 1 on page 44). Place the outside edges of the triangle along the raw edges of the square. Appliqué the triangle in place and cut out the background fabric behind the triangle. Set the remaining triangle aside to use in another project.

Refer to the assembly diagram and stitch together pieces G, H, J, I and C. Then sew the M pieces to the top and bottom of the K pieces. Refer to the diagram and sew the A, B, D, E, L, F and KM pieces together for the front of the house. Appliqué all to the background fabric.

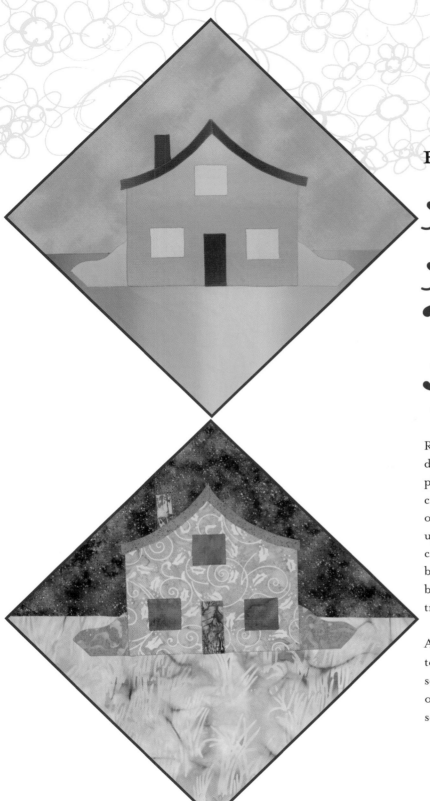

Aunt Amy's Town House

Refer to the templates on page 46 for the cutting directions for the appliqué pieces. You will find the placement diagram there as well. You will also need to cut an 11 7/8" square from green fabric. Cut the square once on the diagonal. You will have two triangles. Line up the raw edges of the triangle with the raw edges of one corner of the background square and appliqué it to the background square. You will need to cut away the background behind the triangle. Use the remaining triangle in another project.

Appliqué the C windows, B door, D roof and E chimney to House A. Pin the house unit to the background square. Then pin the F and F reversed shrubs in place on either side of house. Appliqué all to the background square.

BLOCK 11:
Martha Washington Rose

Refer to the templates on page 47 for the cutting directions for the appliqué pieces. You will find the placement diagram there as well.

Pin the B petals to the background square. Then, place the C and C reversed petals between the B petals. Pin the E stem and D leaf along the edge of the square as shown on page 47. Appliqué all in place. Add the A center pieces last.

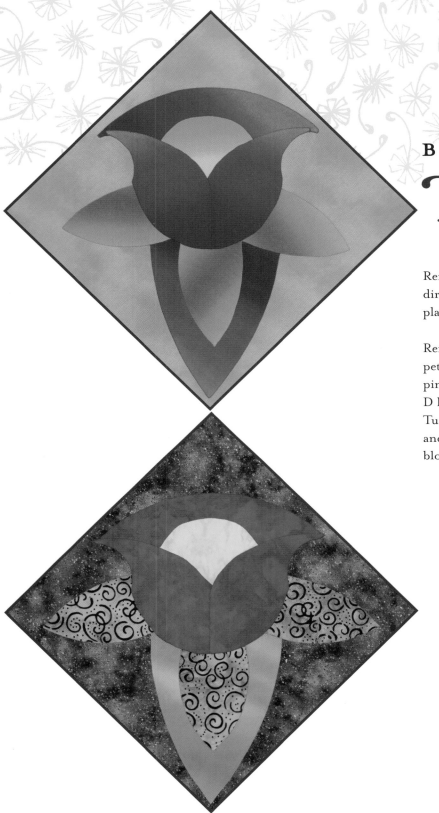

BLOCK 12:
Tulip

Refer to the templates on pages 48-49 for the cutting directions for the appliqué pieces. You will find the placement diagram there as well.

Refer to the diagram on page 49. Begin by sewing the A petal to the tulip center (piece B). Add the C petals and pin the blossom in place. Stitch a small E leaf to the large D leaf. (Refer to the placement diagram if necessary.) Tuck the raw edge of the large D leaf under the C petals and tuck the raw edges of the small E leaves under the blossom. Appliqué all in place to the background square.

BLOCK 13:
Peony

Refer to the templates on pages 50-52 for the cutting directions for the appliqué pieces. You will find the placement diagram there as well.

Sew the G and G reversed pieces to the E and E reversed pieces. Refer to the diagram on page 50 and stitch the bottom portion of the peony together. Pin this portion to the background square. Pin the A and C petals in place, then tuck the B and B reversed leaves in place. Appliqué all to the background square.

Templates

FOLLOW

Dogwood

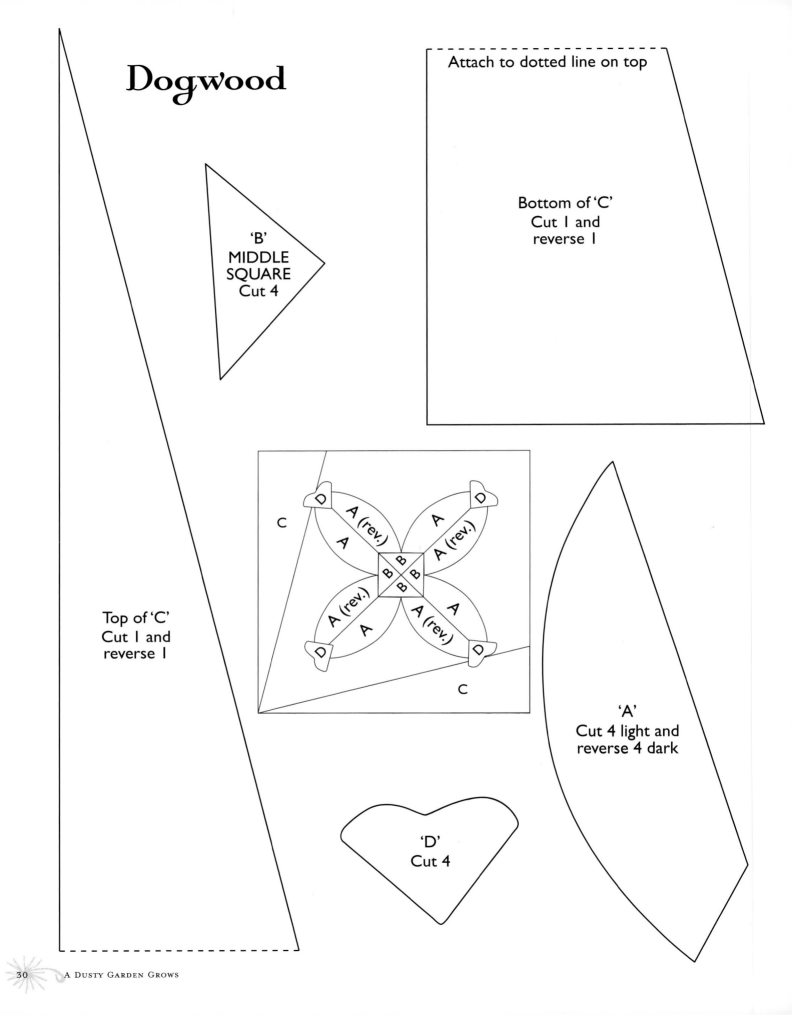

Attach to dotted line on top

Bottom of 'C'
Cut 1 and
reverse 1

'B'
MIDDLE
SQUARE
Cut 4

Top of 'C'
Cut 1 and
reverse 1

C

A (rev.)

A

D

A

A (rev.)

B B
B B

A (rev.)

A

D

A

A (rev.)

D

C

'A'
Cut 4 light and
reverse 4 dark

'D'
Cut 4

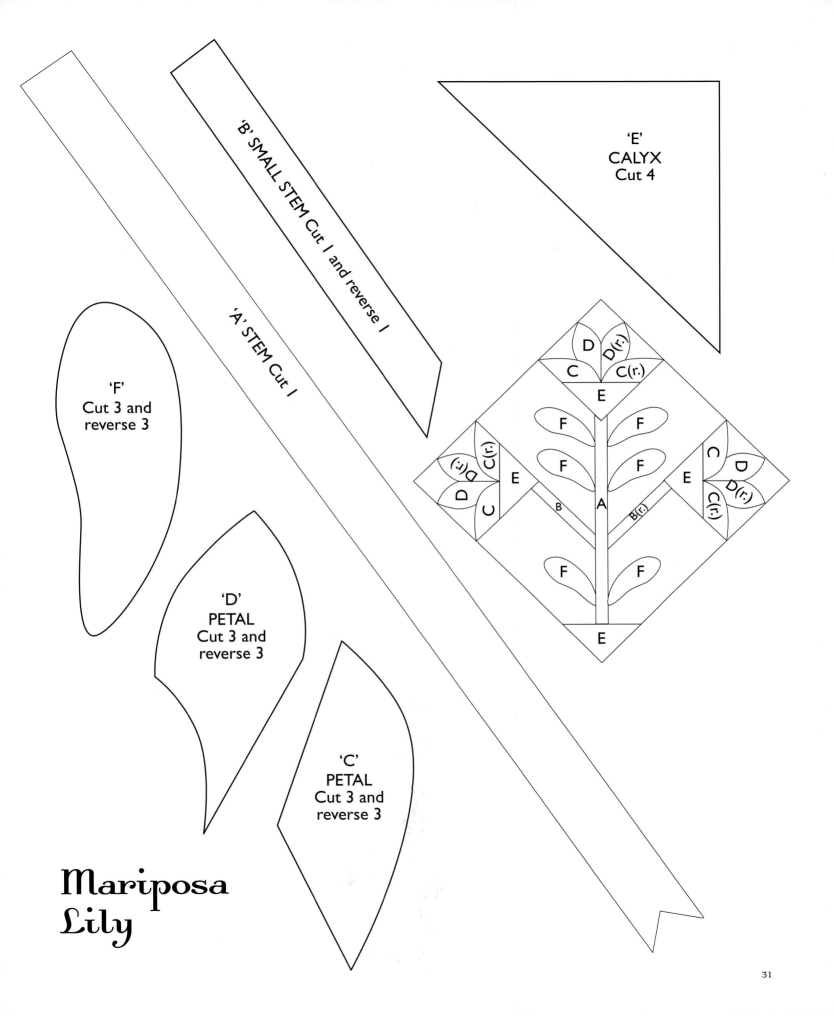

'E'
CALYX
Cut 4

'B' SMALL STEM Cut 1 and reverse 1

'A' STEM Cut 1

'F'
Cut 3 and
reverse 3

'D'
PETAL
Cut 3 and
reverse 3

'C'
PETAL
Cut 3 and
reverse 3

Mariposa
Lily

Calla Lily

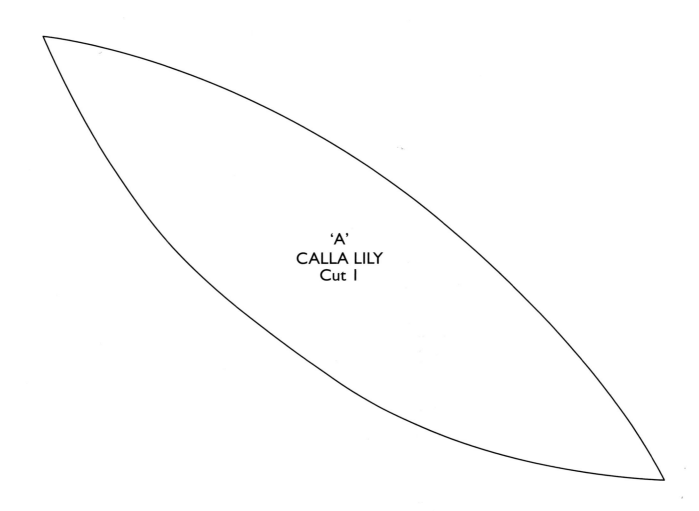

'A'
CALLA LILY
Cut 1

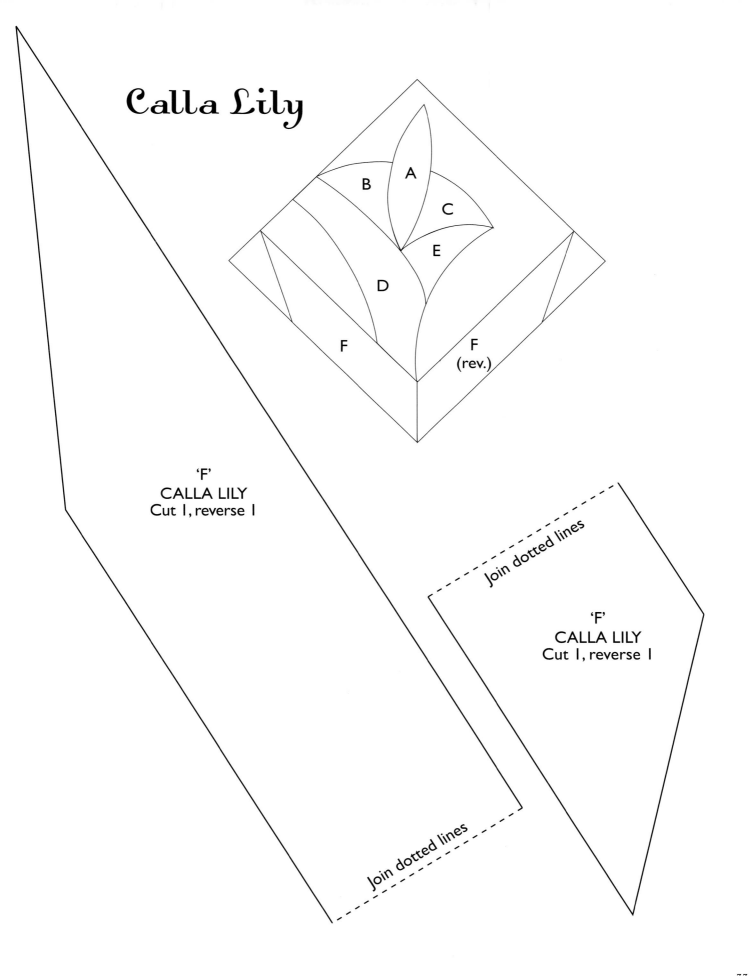

Calla Lily

B

A

C

E

D

F

F
(rev.)

'F'
CALLA LILY
Cut 1, reverse 1

Join dotted lines

'F'
CALLA LILY
Cut 1, reverse 1

Join dotted lines

33

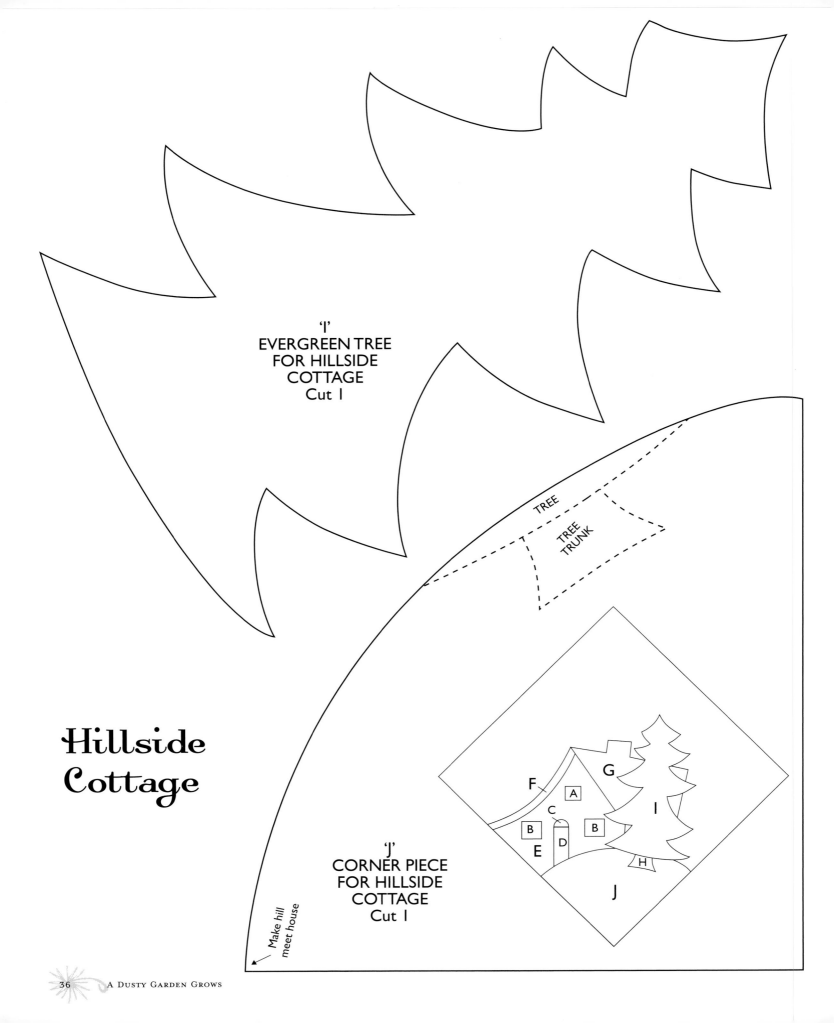

'I'
EVERGREEN TREE
FOR HILLSIDE
COTTAGE
Cut 1

TREE

TREE
TRUNK

Hillside
Cottage

'J'
CORNER PIECE
FOR HILLSIDE
COTTAGE
Cut 1

F

G

A

C

B

B

D

E

I

H

J

Make hill
meet house

Wide Awake School House

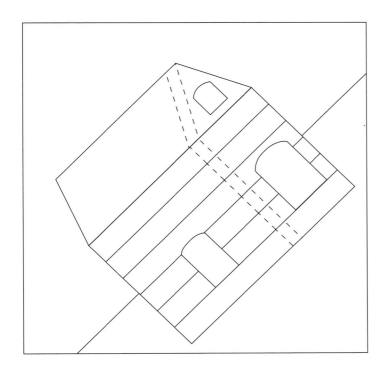

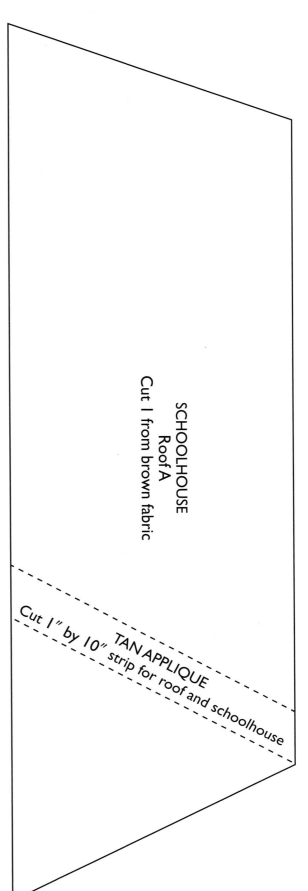

SCHOOLHOUSE
Roof A
Cut 1 from brown fabric

TAN APPLIQUE
Cut 1" by 10" strip for roof and schoolhouse

SCHOOLHOUSE
WINDOW
Window C
Cut 1

SCHOOL-
HOUSE
WINDOW
Window B
Cut 1

SCHOOLHOUSE
DOOR
Cut 1

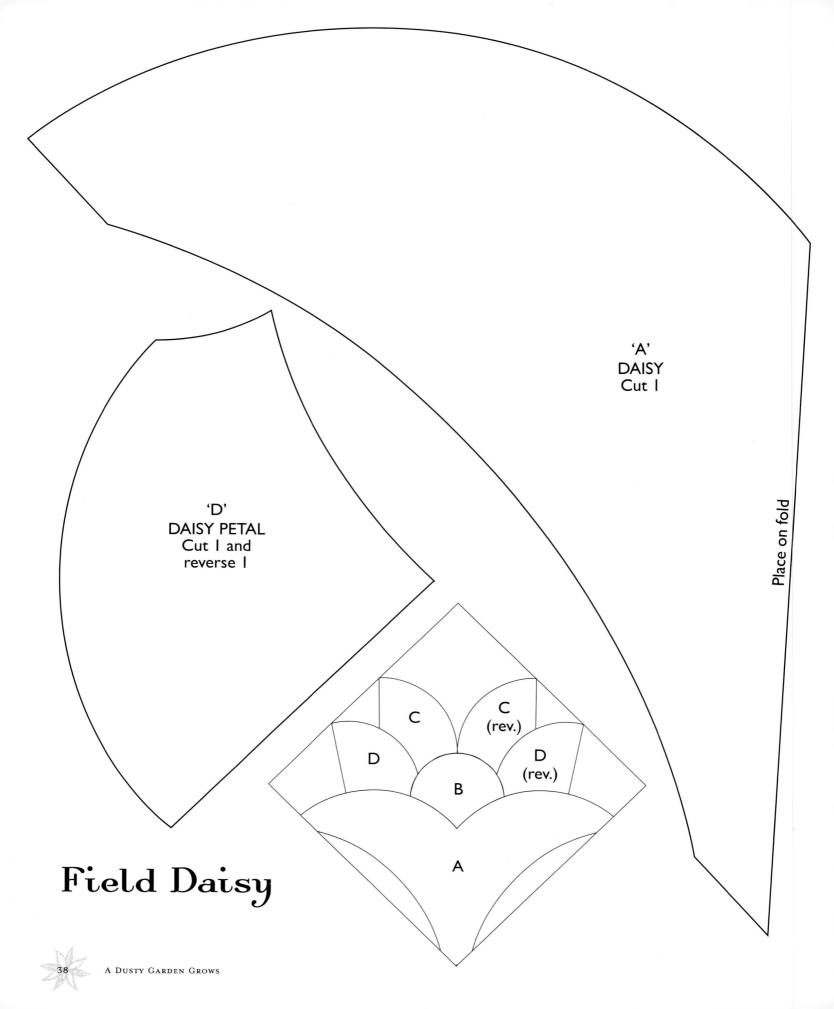

'A'
DAISY
Cut 1

Place on fold

'D'
DAISY PETAL
Cut 1 and
reverse 1

C

C
(rev.)

D

D
(rev.)

B

A

Field Daisy

Field Daisy

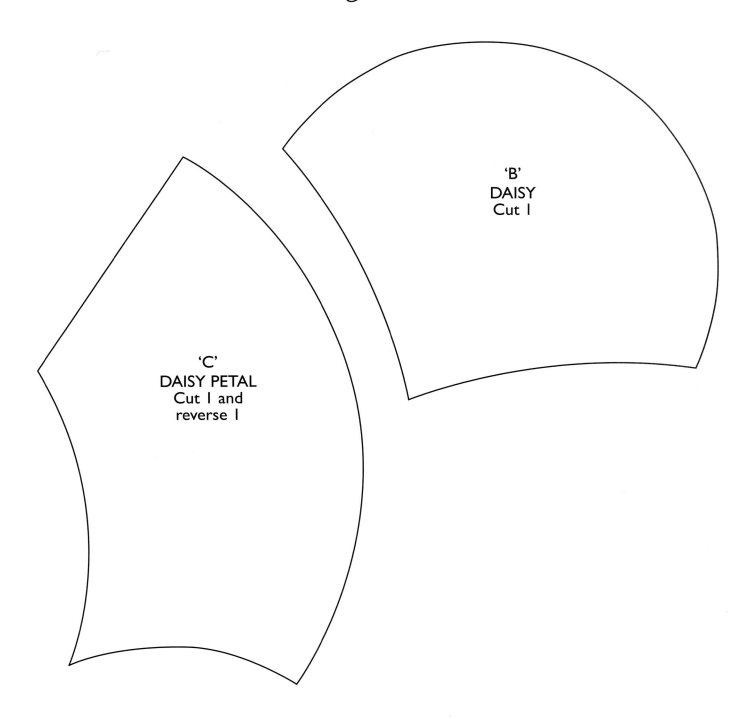

'C'
DAISY PETAL
Cut 1 and
reverse 1

'B'
DAISY
Cut 1

Iris

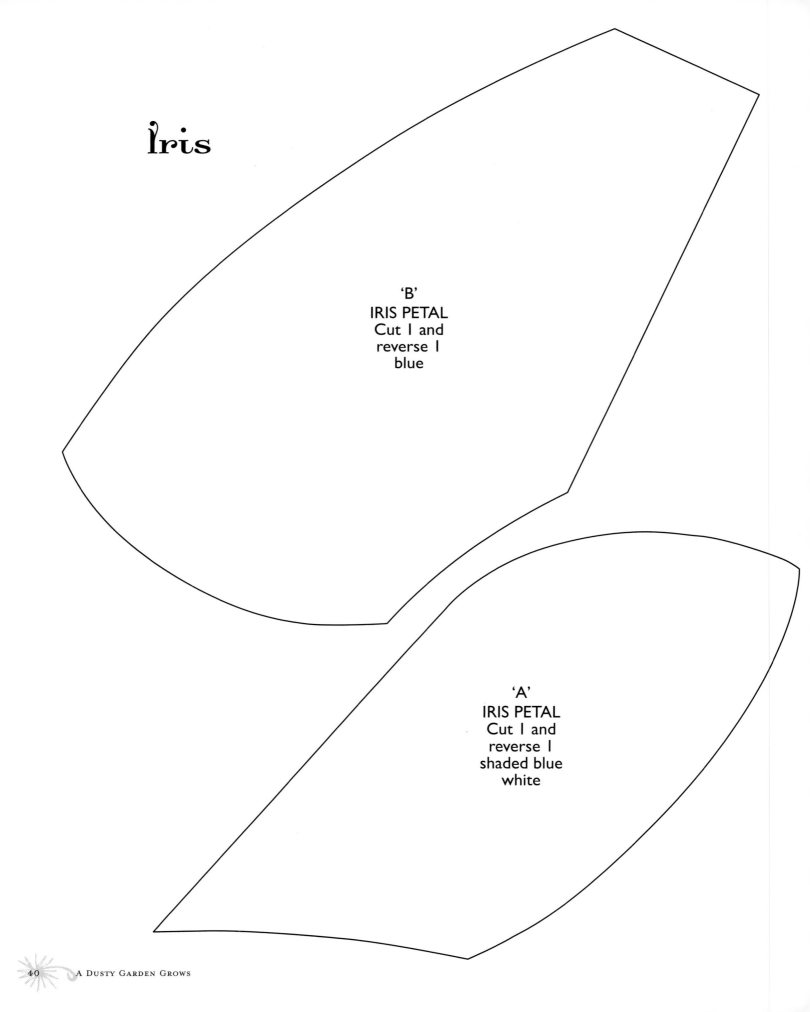

'B'
IRIS PETAL
Cut 1 and
reverse 1
blue

'A'
IRIS PETAL
Cut 1 and
reverse 1
shaded blue
white

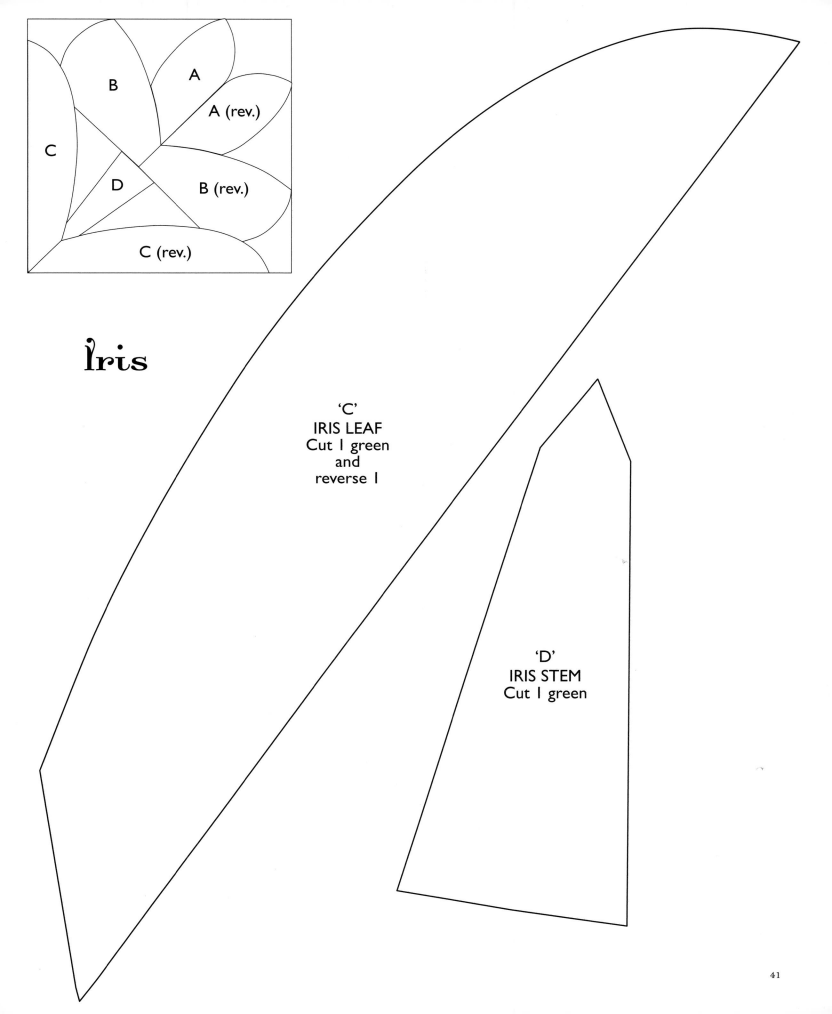

Iris

'C'
IRIS LEAF
Cut 1 green
and
reverse 1

'D'
IRIS STEM
Cut 1 green

Crocus

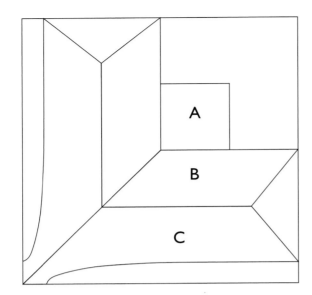

'A'
CROCUS
CENTER
Cut 1

'B'
INNER PETALS
Cut 1, reverse 1

Crocus

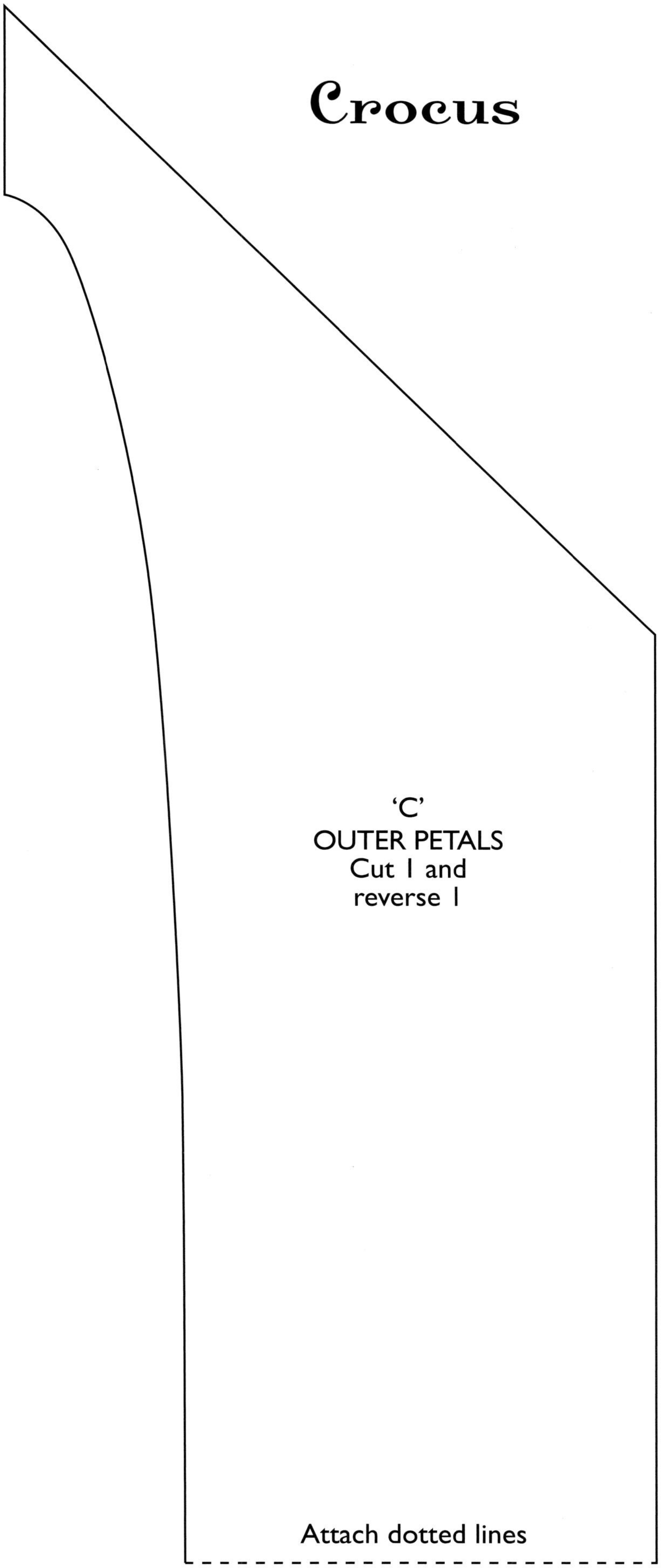

'C'
OUTER PETALS
Cut 1 and
reverse 1

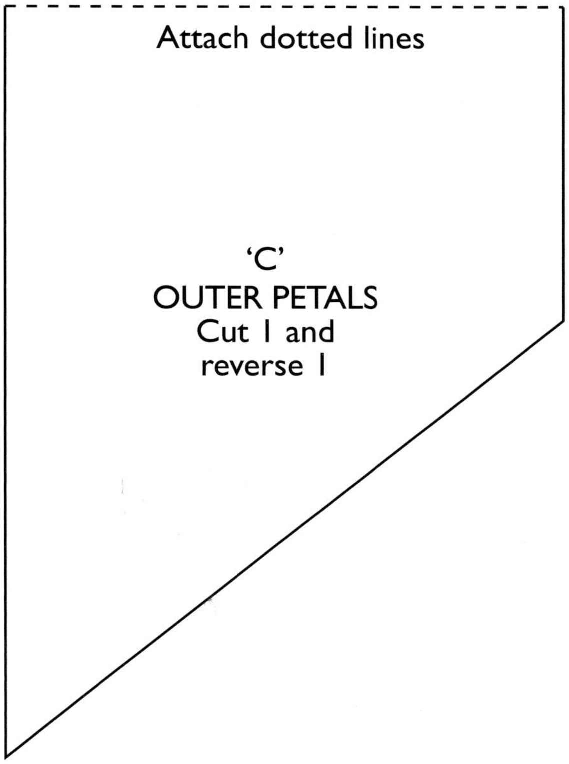

Attach dotted lines

'C'
OUTER PETALS
Cut 1 and
reverse 1

Attach dotted lines

Uncle Wilbur's Home

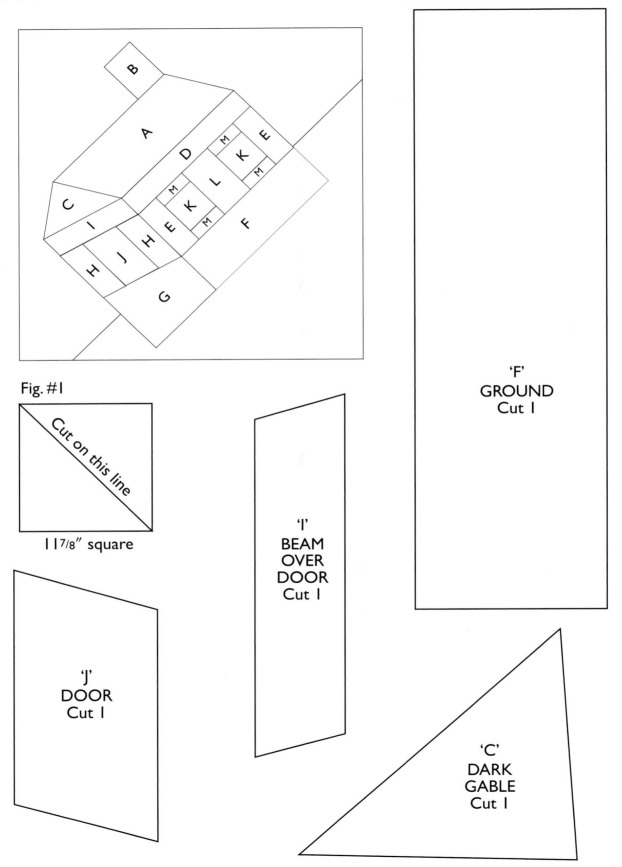

Fig. #1

Cut on this line

11⁷/₈″ square

'F'
GROUND
Cut 1

'I'
BEAM
OVER
DOOR
Cut 1

'J'
DOOR
Cut 1

'C'
DARK
GABLE
Cut 1

Uncle Wilbur's Home

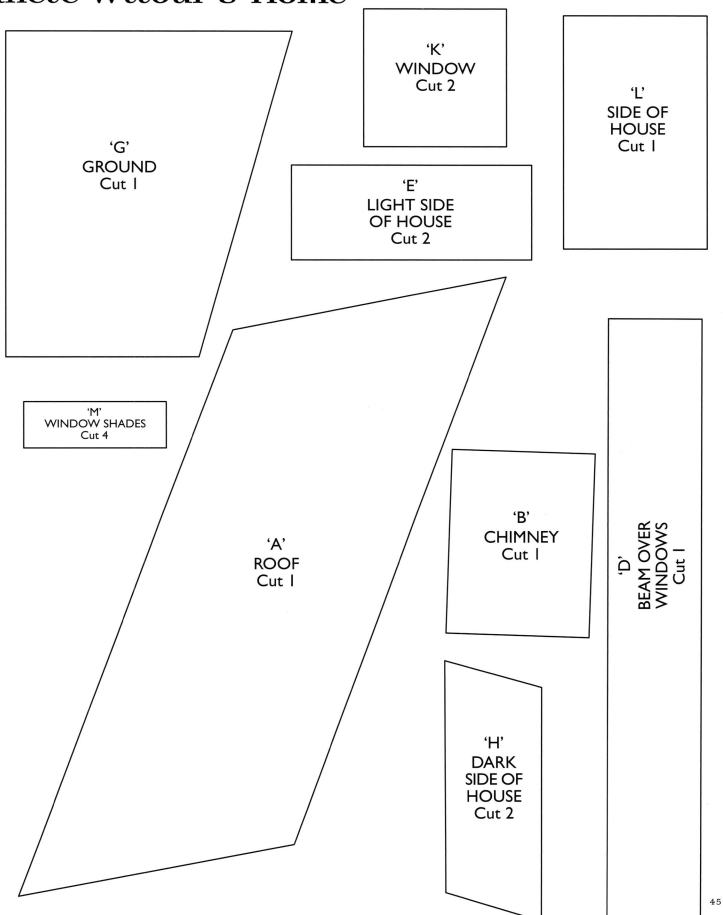

'G'
GROUND
Cut 1

'K'
WINDOW
Cut 2

'L'
SIDE OF
HOUSE
Cut 1

'E'
LIGHT SIDE
OF HOUSE
Cut 2

'M'
WINDOW SHADES
Cut 4

'A'
ROOF
Cut 1

'B'
CHIMNEY
Cut 1

'D'
BEAM OVER
WINDOWS
Cut 1

'H'
DARK
SIDE OF
HOUSE
Cut 2

Aunt Amy's Town House

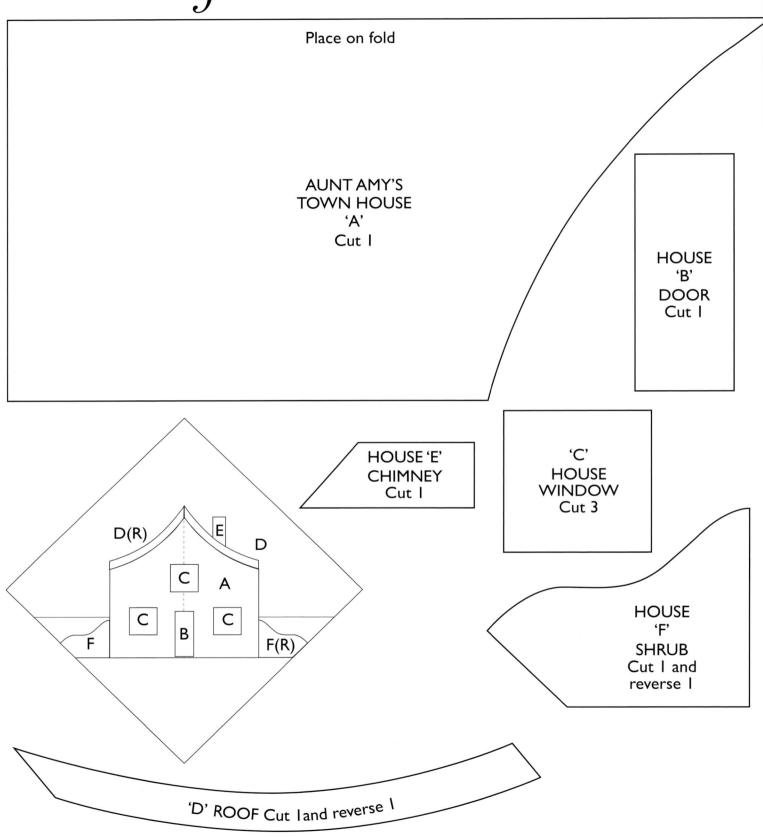

Place on fold

AUNT AMY'S
TOWN HOUSE
'A'
Cut 1

HOUSE
'B'
DOOR
Cut 1

HOUSE 'E'
CHIMNEY
Cut 1

'C'
HOUSE
WINDOW
Cut 3

HOUSE
'F'
SHRUB
Cut 1 and
reverse 1

'D' ROOF Cut 1 and reverse 1

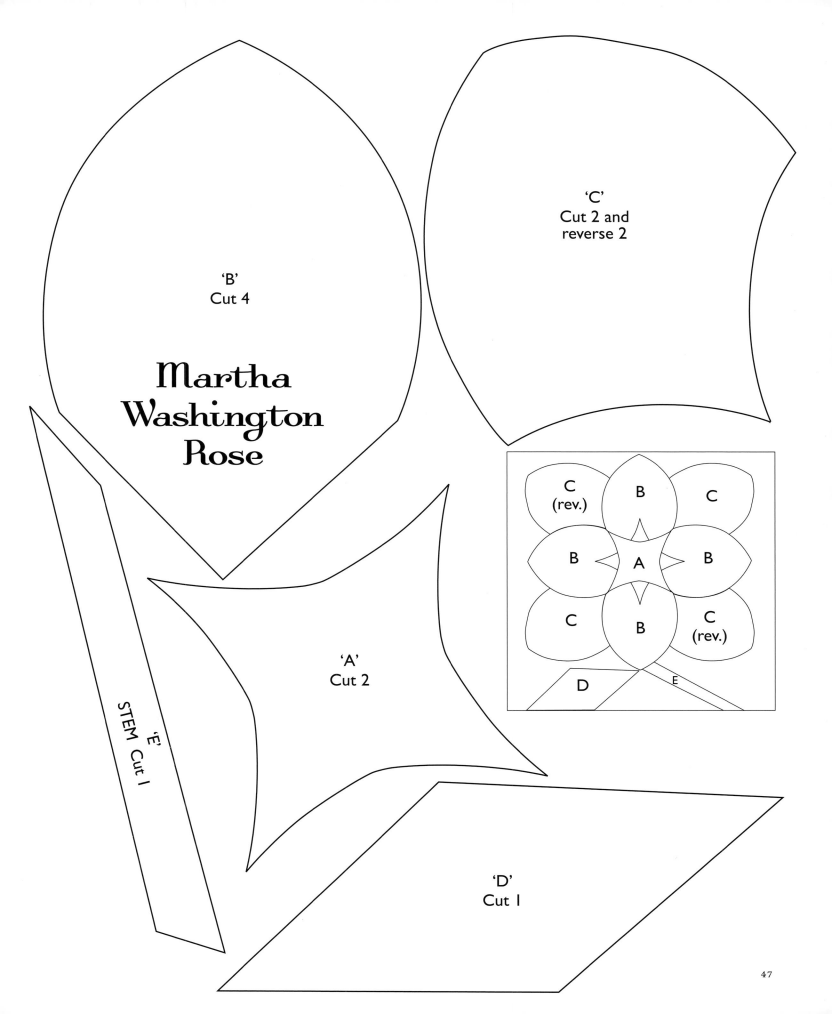

'B'
Cut 4

'C'
Cut 2 and
reverse 2

Martha Washington Rose

'A'
Cut 2

'E'
STEM Cut 1

'D'
Cut 1

C
(rev.)

B

C

B

A

B

C

B

C
(rev.)

D

E

47

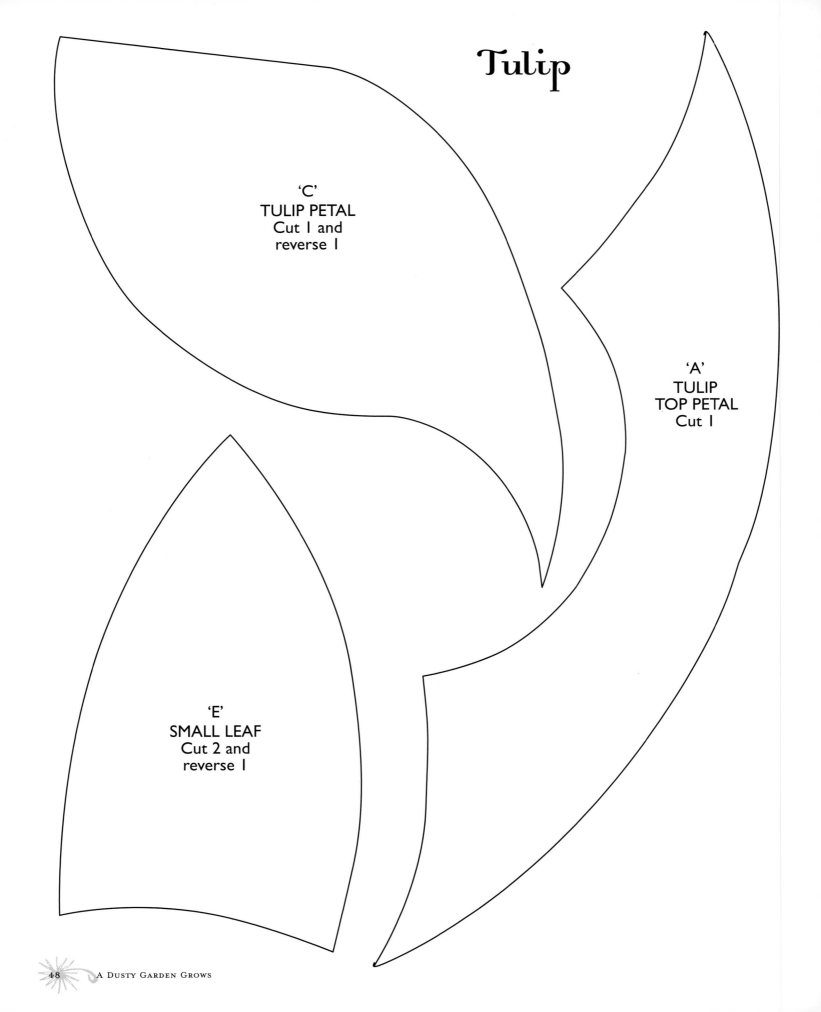

Tulip

'C'
TULIP PETAL
Cut 1 and
reverse 1

'A'
TULIP
TOP PETAL
Cut 1

'E'
SMALL LEAF
Cut 2 and
reverse 1

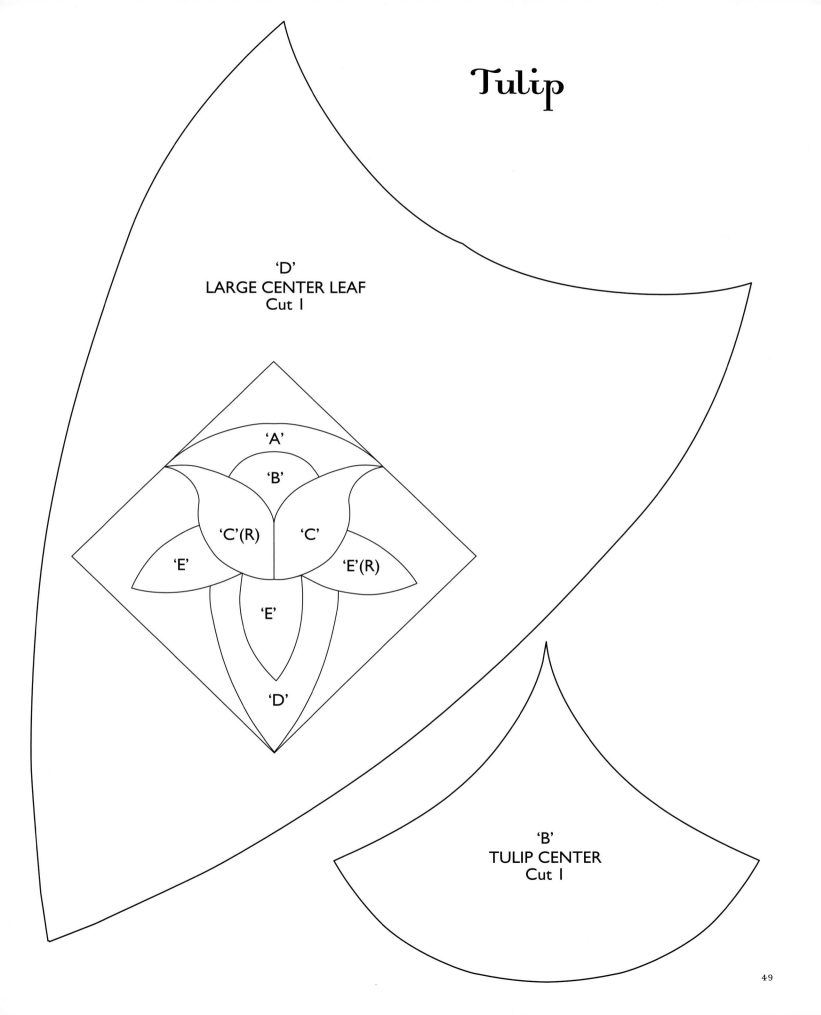

Tulip

'D'
LARGE CENTER LEAF
Cut 1

'A'

'B'

'C'(R)   'C'

'E'   'E'(R)

'E'

'D'

'B'
TULIP CENTER
Cut 1

Peony

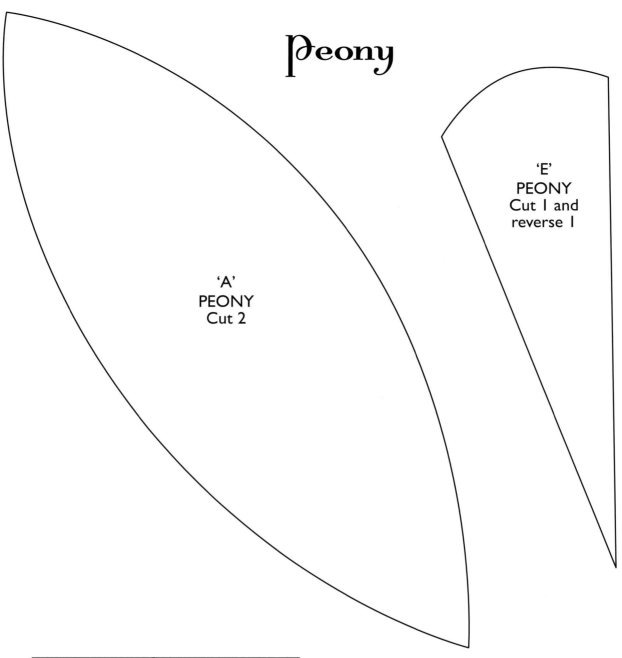

'A'
PEONY
Cut 2

'E'
PEONY
Cut 1 and
reverse 1

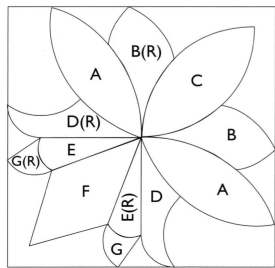

Peony

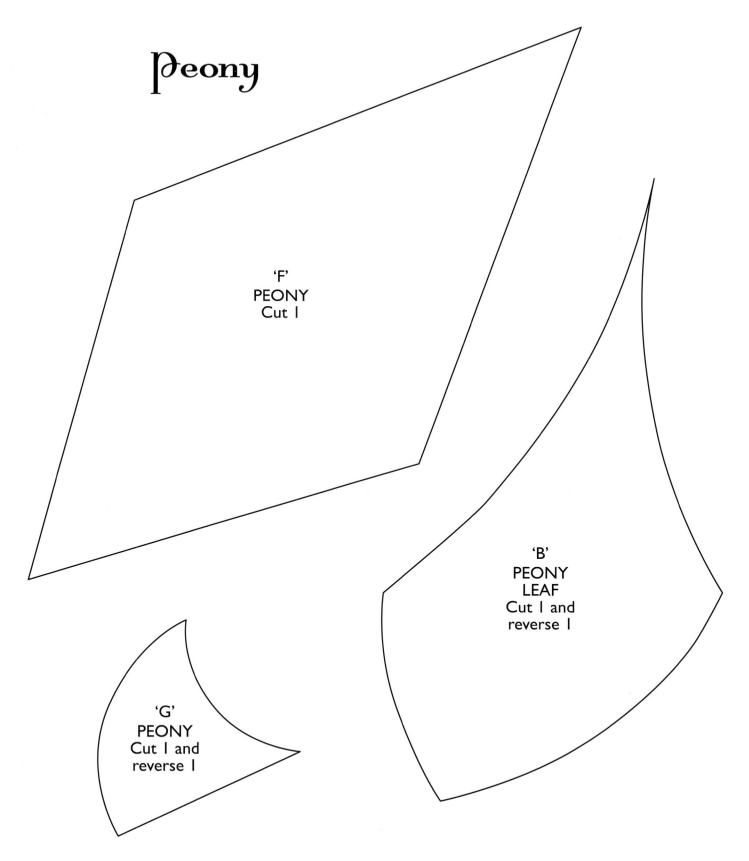

'F'
PEONY
Cut 1

'B'
PEONY
LEAF
Cut 1 and
reverse 1

'G'
PEONY
Cut 1 and
reverse 1

Peony

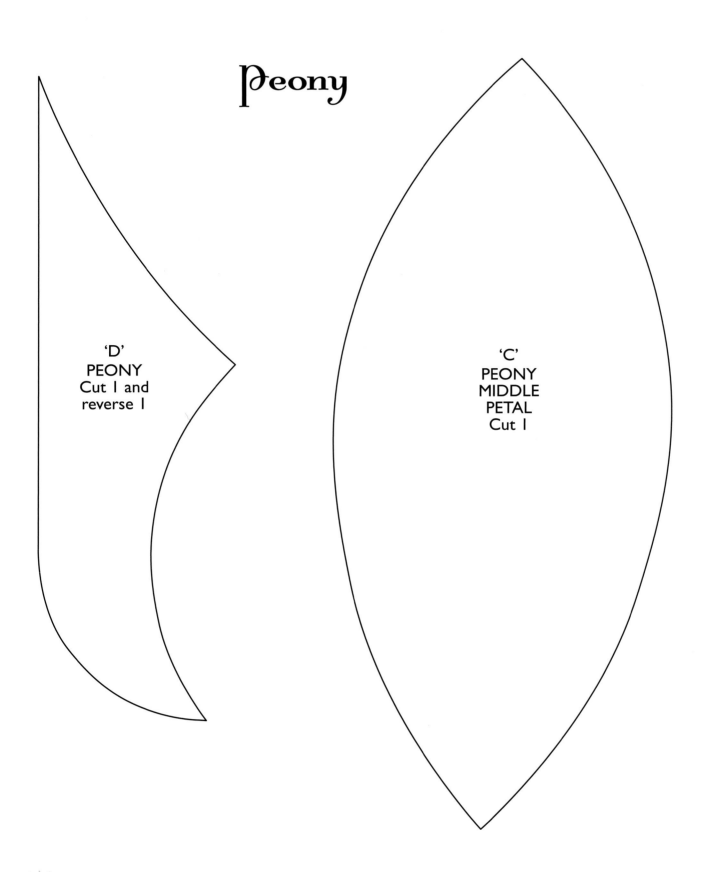

'D'
PEONY
Cut 1 and
reverse 1

'C'
PEONY
MIDDLE
PETAL
Cut 1

Dust Bowl Days

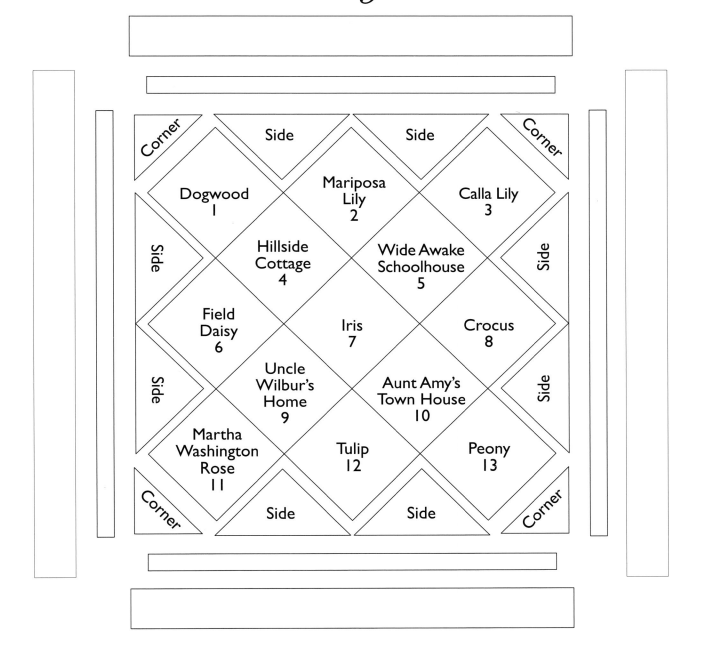

Corner	Side	Side	Corner
Dogwood 1	Mariposa Lily 2	Calla Lily 3	
Hillside Cottage 4	Wide Awake Schoolhouse 5		
Field Daisy 6	Iris 7	Crocus 8	
Uncle Wilbur's Home 9	Aunt Amy's Town House 10		
Martha Washington Rose 11	Tulip 12	Peony 13	
Corner	Side	Side	Corner

Fig. #1
For side setting triangles
Cut two 21$\frac{1}{8}$" brown squares

Fig. #2
For four corner triangles
Cut two 10$\frac{7}{8}$" brown
squares on diagonal

DUST BOWL DAYS ARE OVER

Quilt Size: 86" x 86"

Appliquéd by Jean Stanclift • Quilted by: Eula Lang

Dust Bowl Days Are Over

YARDAGE:

Choose a sky blue background with white clouds of a cheerful blue shaded print or solid. I used Carol Bryer Fallert Gradations.

* 5 yards light blue for 13 - 14 1/2" squares, 8 side setting triangles, and 4 corner triangles.
* 2 1/2 yards for outside border
* 3 yards for sashing and binding - use a shaded light/dark solid
* 1 – 2 fat quarters each of shaded reds, pinks, greens, yellows, purples, oranges, blue, tan and brown for flowers and houses. Use scraps for more variety.

CUTTING DIRECTIONS:

* 13 - 14 1/2" squares from the background fabric.
* 2 - 24 5/8" squares. Cut each square twice on the diagonal to make 8 side setting triangles. See Fig. 2 on the setting diagram on page 56.
* 2 -14 3/8" squares. Cut each square once on the diagonal to make 4 corner triangles. See Fig. 1 on the setting diagram on page 56.
* 9 – 3" strips across the width of the shaded blue fabric. Cut the strips into 14 1/2" lengths for the short sashing. You will need 18 strips.
* 9 – 3" strips across the width of the fabric for the long sashing strips. Sew the strips end to end to make one long strip. From this long strip, cut 2 strips 19 1/2" long, 2 strips 50" long and 2 strips 85 1/2" long.

SEWING DIRECTIONS:

I sewed the blocks in a different setting from the brown quilt but used the same patterns. Follow the same instructions for sewing each flower block as given for the brown quilt.

MORNING GLORIES:

* Cut 4 – 1" x 10" strips for the stems for the corner triangles.
* Cut 8 – 1" x 13" strips for the stems for the side triangles.
* Turn under the seam allowances using a 1/2" clover bias tape maker.
* Cut 18 pink and 18 blue morning glories.
* Cut 3 blossoms and 2 leaves per stem
* Alternate the pink and blue blossoms on each triangle around the quilt. Appliqué the morning glories to each triangle

To set the blocks with the shaded blue sashing, I placed the blocks on point on a design wall with a 2 1/2" space between the blocks. I alternated the light and dark blue parts of the sashing at the top and bottom of each block. I also alternated and matched the corners of each block where it meets the next row. Sew the short sashing strips to the blocks.

SETTING THE FINISHED SQUARES:

Follow the setting diagram on page 56 and sew each row of blocks together on the diagonal. Begin and end the rows with a side setting triangle where indicated. Follow the setting diagram and add in the long sashing strips where indicated. Add the corner triangles after all the rows are sewn together.

Measure the quilt through the center and cut enough 6 1/2" strips of blue for the border.

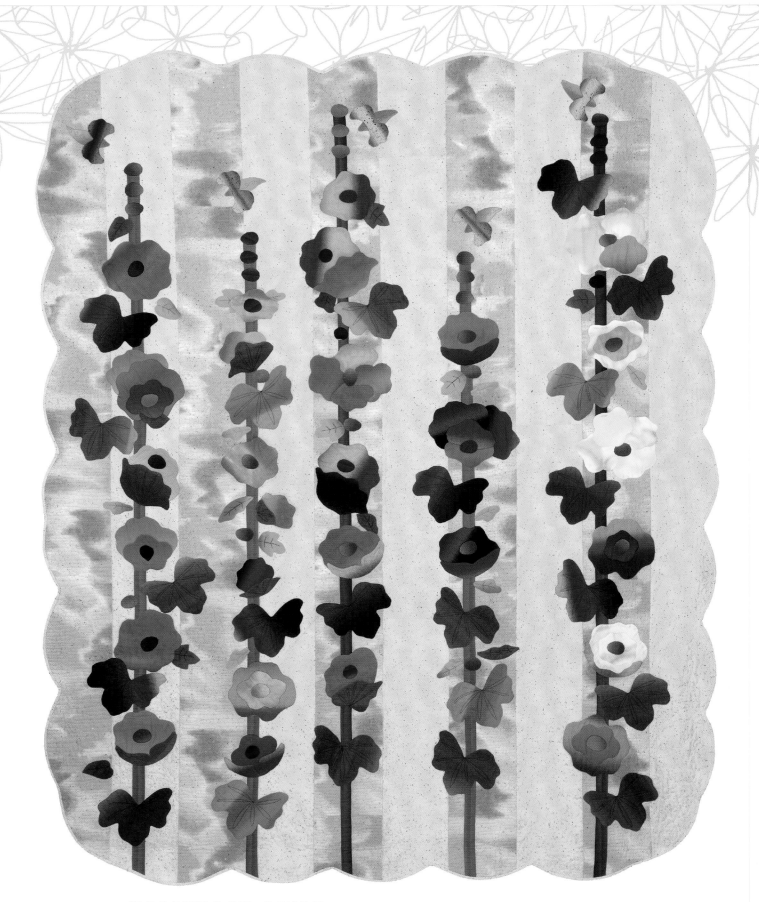

HOLLYHOCK QUILT
Size: 60" x 75"
Owned by Terry Clothier Thompson.

Hollyhock Quilt

SIZE: 60" X 75"

Hollyhocks are a popular biennial cottage garden flower that reseeds every year, comes in a variety of lovely colors and grows up to 6 feet tall. Drive down the alleys of older neighborhoods in your town, and you will see them still growing and blooming at the edges of once glorious Victorian gardens.

Little girls once made doll dresses of the large blooms and hats for their china head dolls. Hollyhocks surrounded the "privy" so visiting, shy Victorian ladies would only have to ask "Where are the Hollyhocks?" and be directed to the privy without having to actually say the word in polite company.

Enjoy sewing Terry's vision of her garden's Hollyhocks. She chose shaded fabrics to give the illusion of sunlight moving through the flowerbed. The flowers in this quilt bloom year round and bring cheer to gloomy days.

Terry chose shaded fabrics for all flowers, leaves and stems. Batiks would also look great! The shading gives more dimension and lifelike shapes.

YARDAGE

* 2 yards sky-blue print
* 3 yards yellow print - dots, specks or tiny floral
* 1/3 yard green for stems
* 1/2 yard each of shaded blue, violet, red, orange, pink, yellow, brown, gold, greens, for flowers, leaves, calyx, ovals and moths.
* 1"Clover bias maker for stems
* 5 yards for backing
* No. 2 lead pencil for marking scallops
* Optional: "The Original Vine Line," a marking tool designed by Terry for making vines and scalloped edges. Check with your quilt shop or Terry's web site.

DIRECTIONS

CUTTING AND ASSEMBLING BACKGROUND

* Cut all strips on the cross-grain, selvedge to selvedge.
* 10 - 6 1/2"x 42"strips of blue
* 10 – 6 1/2"x 42"strips of yellow

Sew the blue strips together end to end and the yellow strips together end to end. You will have one long blue and one long yellow length of fabric that should measure 6 1/2"x 420" less seam allowances. To prevent all the seams from being lined up across the quilt you will want to stagger them. You can do this by cutting off 6" from the top of the yellow length. Do not do this to the blue length. Now cut the yellow length into 5 - 75 1/2"strips. Cut the blue length into five 75 1/2"strips. This includes seam allowances.

CONTINUED ON NEXT PAGE

CONTINUED FROM PAGE 59.

Sew the strips together. Begin with a blue strip and alternate the colors thus making the background for the quilt. Pin the strips together and be careful not to pull or stretch them when sewing.

MARKING THE SCALLOPED EDGES

If you choose to scallop the edges of the quilt, now is the time to mark the scallops around the edge of the quilt background. It is easier to do this now than when the appliqués are placed.

Press a line 1 3/4" in from the raw edge of the background all the way around the quilt. This is your guideline for marking the shallow scallop. Find the center of each side of the background and mark it with a pin. Either measure each side of the quilt and divide by 2 or simply fold the quilt in half to find the center.

You may want to use a "Vine Line" tool to help you mark the scallops or you can make a plastic template of the scallop pattern provided. Be sure to mark the center line on your template.

Begin by placing the template's center mark and the bottom of the template on the center of one quilt side and the pressed 1 3/4" line. Draw around the curve. Mark all sides by moving the template along the folded line and marking each curve. Continue marking all sides of the quilt. Stop marking before you go around the corners. You will have to fudge the corners in order for the scallops to meet. DO NOT cut the scallops yet. See the binding directions.

APPLIQUÉING THE STEMS

The placement of long stems is easier if you draw a straight line in pencil for a guideline. Refer to the photo if necessary.

To prepare the stems, cut on the cross-grain and piece together for the following stem lengths: NOTE: Pre-washed fabric presses and holds a crease better than unwashed fabric.

✳ 1 stem 2"x 60"
✳ 1 stem 2"x 70"
✳ 1 stem 2"x 65"
✳ 2 stems 2"x 42"

Use the 1" Clover bias tape maker and pull the strips through the tool. Press as you go.

Starting at the bottom of the quilt, place the prepared stems along the pencil line. Allow 1" of the stem to hang over the edge of the quilt. After sewing the stems in place, these "tails" may be cut off. Pin and baste, or glue the stems along the pencil line. Appliqué to the background by hand or machine. Trim off the "tails."

Refer to the picture and create 30 flowers. Plan and utilize all blossoms, calyx and centers. Mix the flowers as you like. Create larger Hollyhocks by combining 3 smaller flowers into a larger flower. You will need to add seam allowances to the appliqué pattern pieces.

Prepare all appliqués for either hand or machine appliqué.

Assemble the flowers and attach the calyx and center
ovals. The ovals may also be used as seedpods at the top
of and along the stems. Place and pin the flowers, seeds
and leaves on the stems before sewing. Use the photo as a
placement guide and add more leaves and seeds where
you want them. You may want to pin, baste and sew one
stem at a time if that is easiest for you.

Assemble the 5 moths. Place, pin and sew them above
the Hollyhocks.

Quilt the Hollyhock quilt by hand or machine right out
to the edges of the quilt, over the penciled scallops.

Make bias binding from the yellow fabric for the quilt.
Sew the edge of the binding along the scalloped pencil
line going into the slight curves of the connecting
scallops. As you turn the needle into the curve, there will
be a slight pucker. After the entire binding is sewn to the
top, cut away the top, batting and backing. Roll the
binding over the edge of the quilt and whip-stitch it to
the back.

Hollyhocks

Fig. #1

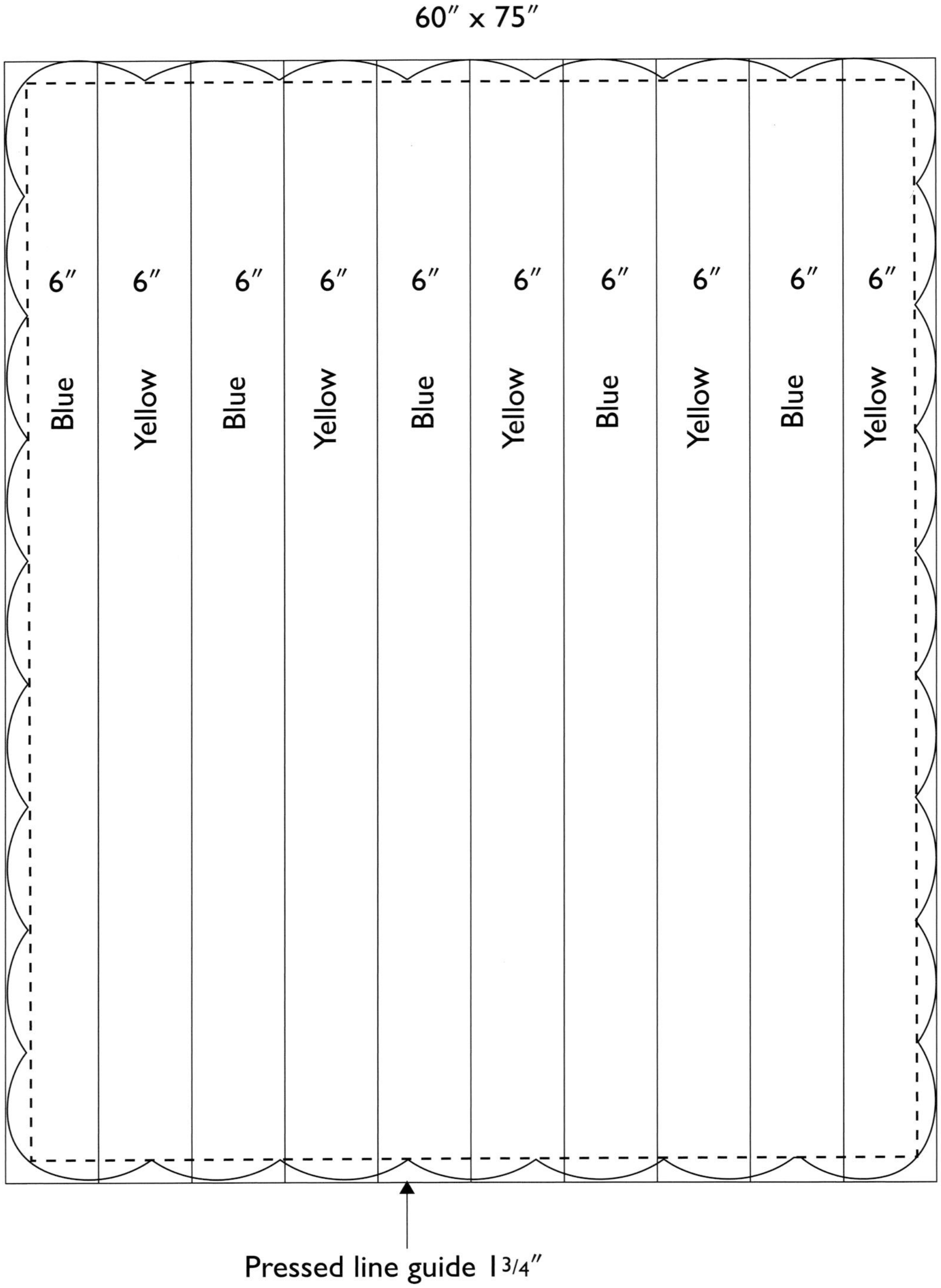

60″ x 75″

	6″	6″	6″	6″	6″	6″	6″	6″	6″	6″
	Blue	Yellow	Blue	Yellow	Blue	Yellow	Blue	Yellow	Blue	Yellow

Pressed line guide 1¾″

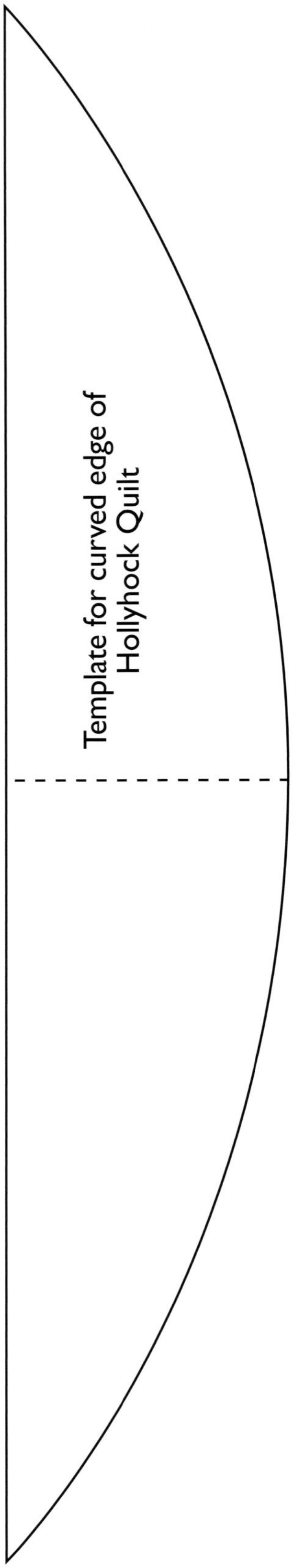

Template for curved edge of Hollyhock Quilt

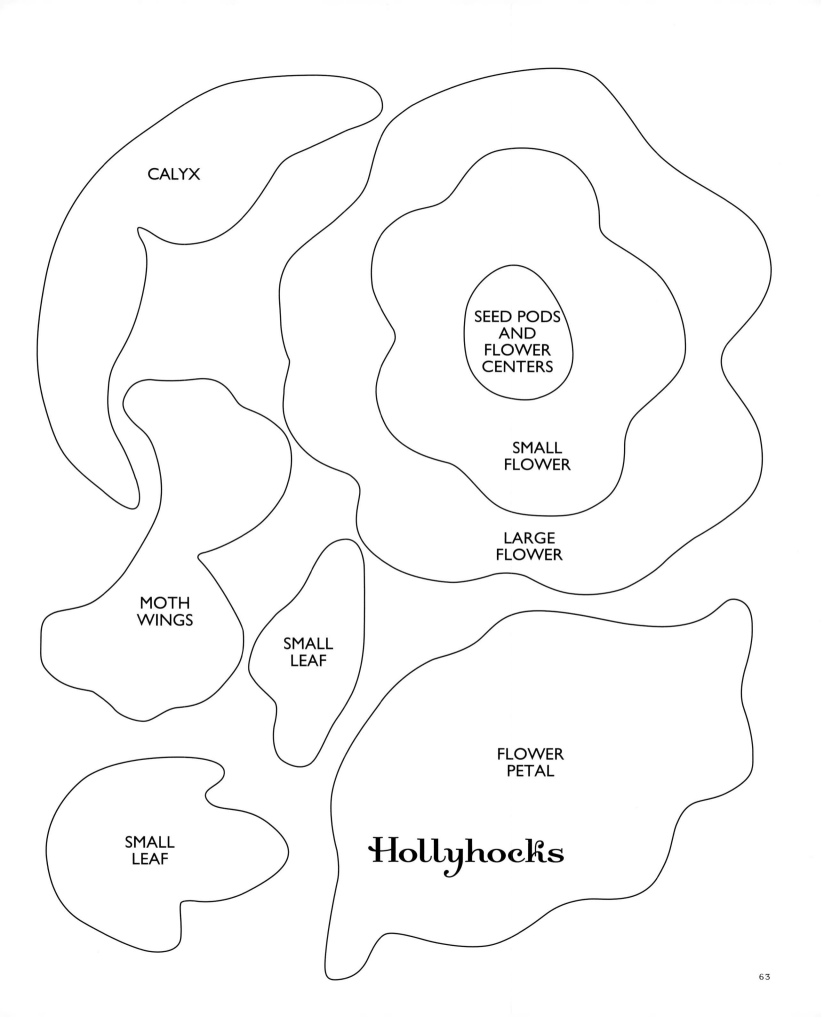

CALYX

SEED PODS
AND
FLOWER
CENTERS

SMALL
FLOWER

LARGE
FLOWER

MOTH
WINGS

SMALL
LEAF

FLOWER
PETAL

SMALL
LEAF

Hollyhocks

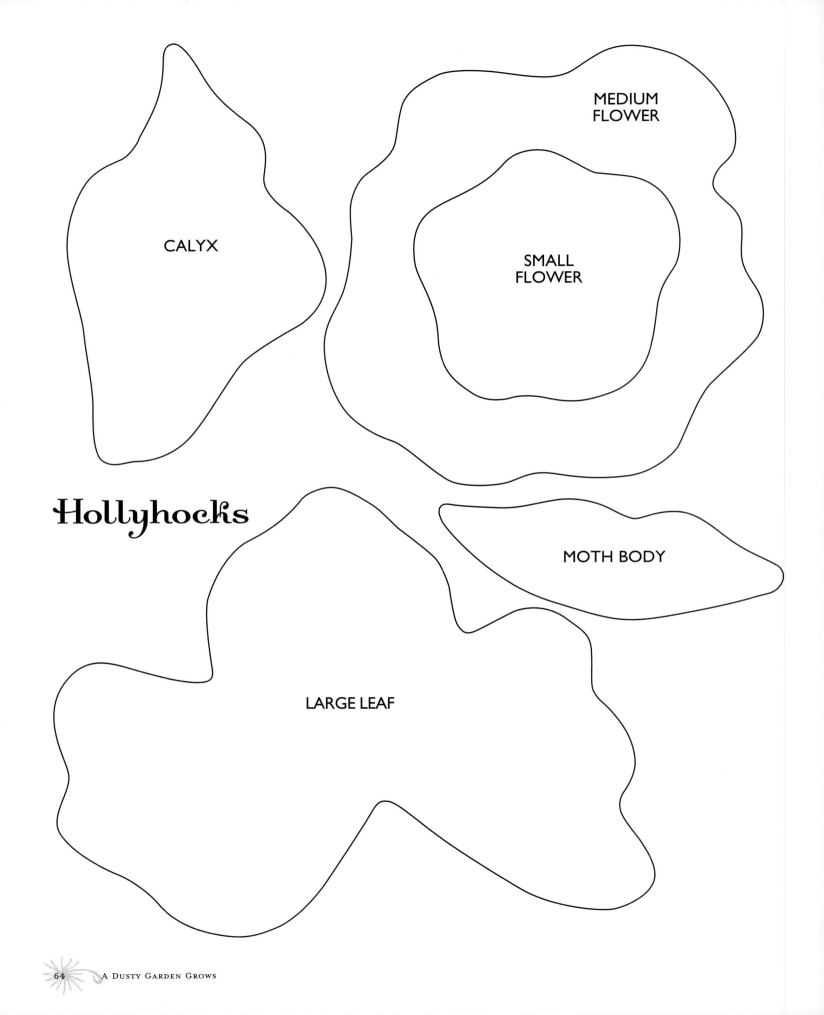

CALYX

MEDIUM
FLOWER

SMALL
FLOWER

Hollyhocks

MOTH BODY

LARGE LEAF

Snapdragons

Snapdragons bloomed in Mrs. Nail's flowerbeds, giving off a faint, sweet fragrance. Lavender and purple violets filled the shady spots near the flagstones.

—Patricia Wilson Clothier

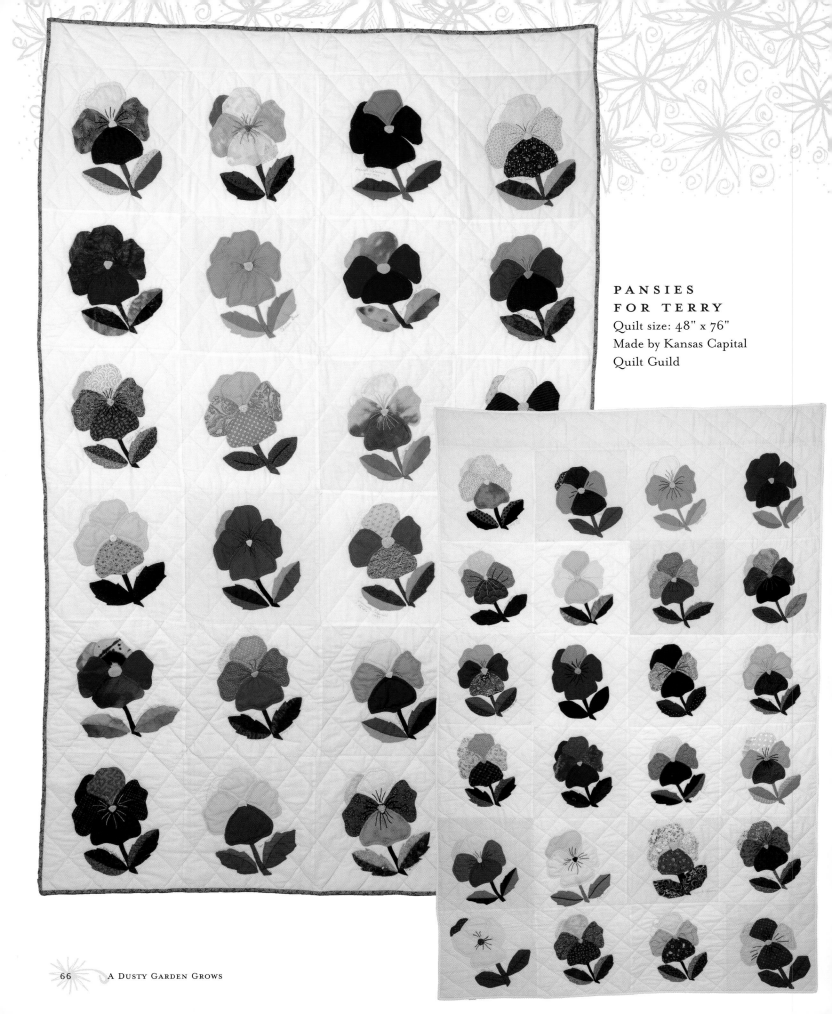

**PANSIES
FOR TERRY**
Quilt size: 48" x 76"
Made by Kansas Capital
Quilt Guild

Pansies for Terry

SIZE: 48" X 76"

YARDAGE:

* 3 1/2 yards white or ecru for background squares and top border.
* 16 fat quarters of shaded blues, greens, yellows, reds, pinks, purples and golds for pansies, stems and leaves. Using shaded fabrics and batiks gives a natural look to the flowers and leaves. Mix reds and pinks, golds and blues, purples and golds. Pansies have a beautiful and varied mixed palette of colors so have fun creating your own combinations.
* 3/4 yard fabric for binding.

CUTTING INSTRUCTIONS:

Cut:

* 24 - 12 1/2" squares from background fabric.
* Cut 24 flower petals using templates A, B, C, D, E and I for the flowers
* 24 stems using template H
* 24 leaf F
* 24 leaf F reversed
* 24 leaf G
* 24 leaf G reversed

Prepare all pieces for appliqué by hand or machine.

Piece the leaves with 2 shades of green.

Place each pansy on a background square. Baste in place, overlapping the petals as shown on page 68 with dotted lines.

Embroider the lines in the petals with black perle cotton or embroidery floss.

Appliqué the I center piece in place.

Set the finished blocks together as shown on page 69.

Sew a 4 1/2" white or ecru border to the top of quilt. Quilt in the ditch in the seams of the pansies then echo around each blossom. Quilt 3" diagonal squares in the background of the block.

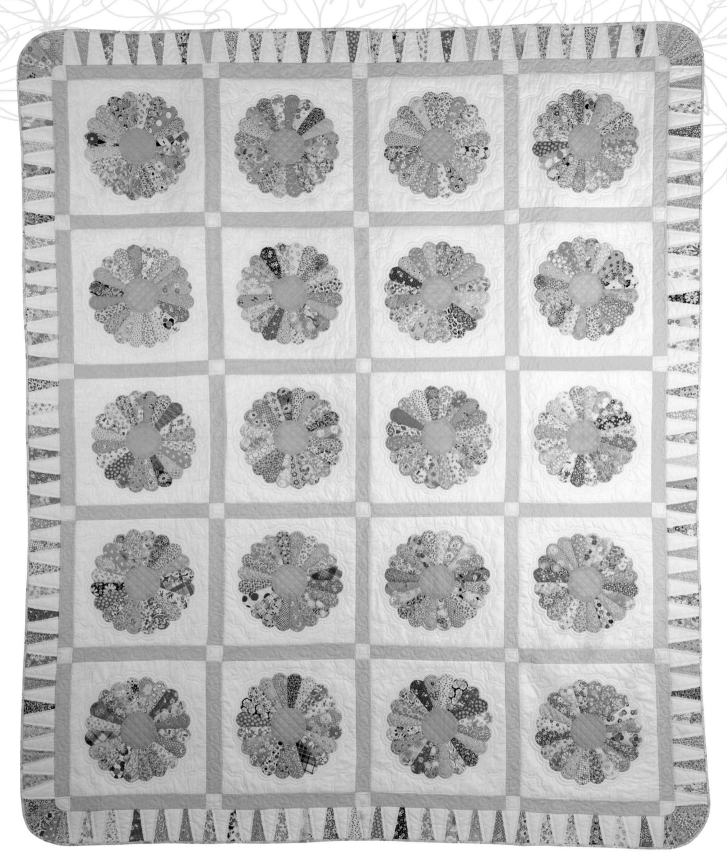

DRESDEN PLATE C. 1930–1940

Quilt size: 78"x 95"

Top owned by Terry Clothier Thompson · Machine quilted by Lori Kukuk

Dresden Plate

SIZE: 78" X 95"

YARDAGE:

For a 1930-1940s look quilt, you may choose any pastel color for a background and still be in keeping with the time period.

* 4 1/2 yards of white or ecru for 20 - 15" finished squares
* 3 1/3 yards of yellow for sashing, binding and center circles
* 1 1/2 yards white for D wedges and cornerstones
* For the plate wedges, buy fat quarters or quarter yard cuts of 20 different 1930s reproduction prints. For a "use it all up" look, use scraps. If you want a different look, try shaded fabrics or batiks for the A wedges. You will need 400 A wedges for 20 blocks and 20 A wedges for the 4 curved corners.
* For the top and bottom pieced borders, you will need 48 C print wedges and 50 white D wedges. For the 2 side borders, you will need 60 print C wedges and 62 white D wedges.

CUTTING DIRECTIONS:

* Cut 20 - 4" circles for centers of plates. (Template B)
* Cut 20 - 15 1/2" squares for background blocks.
* Cut 49 - 2 1/2" yellow strips for sashing.
* Cut 30 - 2 1/2" white squares for sashing cornerstones.
* Cut out all wedges for blocks and borders.

SEWING DIRECTIONS:

Piece 20 A wedges together to make the plate. Make 20 plates. Center each plate on a 15 1/2" background square and appliqué in place. Appliqué the circle over the center of the plates. See Fig. 2 on page 72.

Set the finished blocks together as shown in the diagram on page 74.

For the borders, piece the D and C wedges together. Begin and end each strip with a white wedge and alternate the print and white wedges. Refer to the photo for placement. Measure the inside of the quilt to make sure the pieced border fits the quilt. You can adjust the border by taking the seam allowances in if it is too long or letting a few of them out if it is a bit short. Pin the pieced border to the quilt. Stitch the top and bottom borders in place. Begin sewing about 4"-5" away from the corner and quit sewing about 4"– 5" away from the next corner. Repeat this for the two side borders. All corners should be loose.

Make the 4 corners units by piecing 5 A wedges together. At this time you will want to press the seam allowance under on the short curves. Pin a corner unit to each end of the top and bottom strip. Make sure your border lies flat then sew the seam, adjusting if necessary. It is now time to close up the seam allowance that was left open. Appliqué the small curved edge to the outside cornerstone. Repeat for all four corners.

Quilt the blocks with 3 echo rows around the top of plates. Quilt a 3/4" crosshatch grid in the yellow center circles. For the 4 corners of the block, quilt one-fourth of a rosette. Use the rosette (page 93) in the Colonial Rose quilt for a quilting design template. For the sashing, quilt a trailing vine and leaf design. The border wedges are quilted 1/4" in a straight line from the seam allowance.

Bind with 2" bias binding.

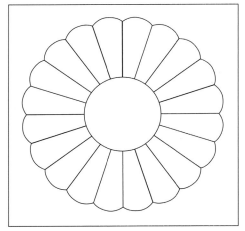

Fig. #2

Dresden Plate

4" CIRCLE
'B'

'A'
WEDGE
Cut 400
prints for
blocks and
20 for
border
corners

'C'
WEDGE
Cut 108 prints
for borders

'WHITE'
BORDER
WEDGE for
Dresden Plate
'D'
Cut 112

Dresden Plate

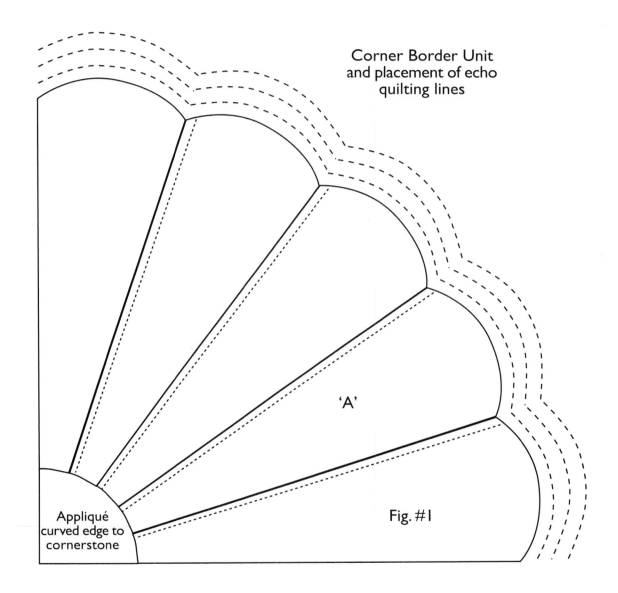

Corner Border Unit
and placement of echo
quilting lines

'A'

Fig. #1

Appliqué
curved edge to
cornerstone

Dresden Plate

15"

Aunt Amy's Kitchen Towel

16" X 37"

YARDAGE:

✳ 1 1/8 yard of brown and tan ticking
✳ For house, 12" x 12" print and scraps of red and green
for windows, roof, door and shrubs.

CUTTING AND
SEWING DIRECTIONS:

✳ Cut a 16 1/2" x 37 1/2" rectangle from the brown and
tan ticking. Hem all the edges.
✳ Cut out the pieces of the house, windows, doors, roof
and chimney. Pin the house a few inches from the
hemmed edge of the bottom of the towel. Appliqué the
pieces in place. Ink or embroider the panes in the
windows.

Bluebonnets

*Bluebonnets carpeted
the shoulders of the dirt roads headed
west. Great patches of the royal blue
blooms balanced the creams and reds
of the clays near Study Butte
and the beiges of Terlingua Creek.*
—Patricia Wilson Clothier

Our long-proposed telephone line
is at last a reality. Those to whom
such service has long been
commonplace can hardly realize
all that is suggested to scattered,
lonely people by the singing wires
and the possibility
of this daily miracle.
—CAROLYN HENDERSON

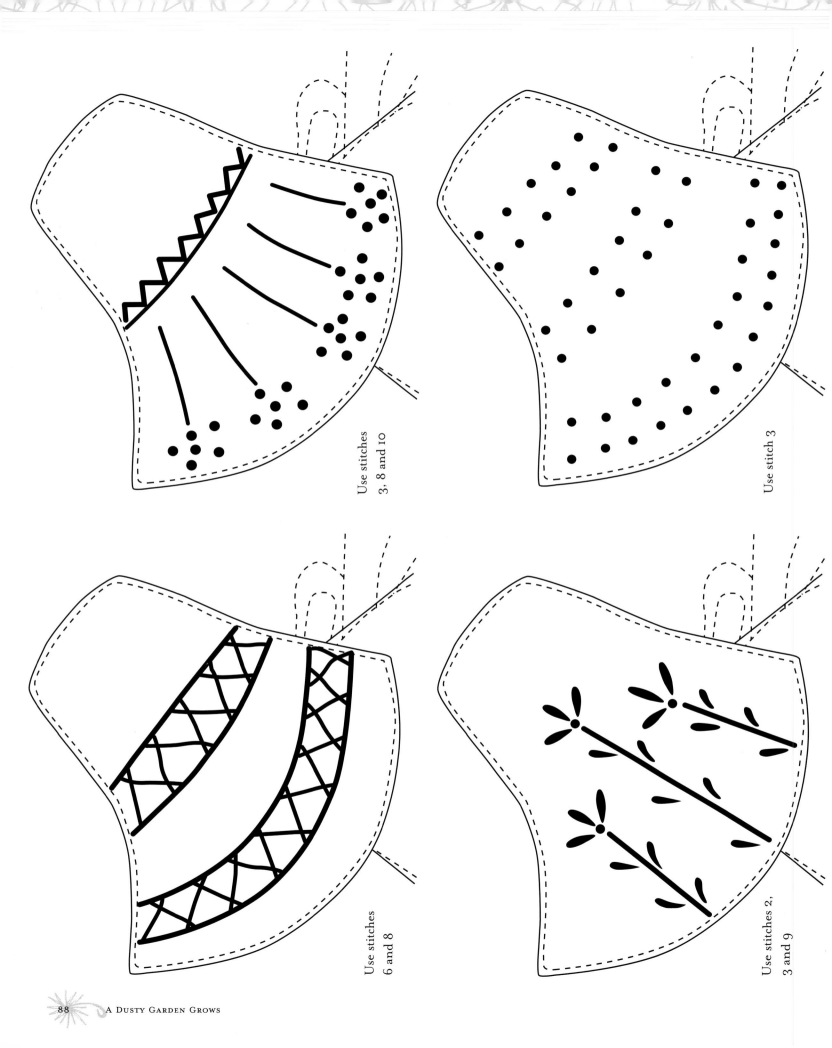

Use stitches
3, 8 and 10

Use stitch 3

Use stitches
6 and 8

Use stitches 2,
3 and 9

Sue Lives
Layout

1 1/2"

1 1/2"

1 1/2"

1 1/2"

1 1/2"

Use stitch 8

COLONIAL ROSE
Quilt Size: 84" x 84"
Owned by Terry Clothier Thompson; Maker Unknown; c.1930 - 1950

Colonial Rose

SIZE: 84" X 84"

YARDAGE REQUIREMENTS:

Yardage based on 42" wide fabric

* 6 1/2 yards ecru for background and borders
* 3 yards light green for swags, calyx, leaves and binding
* 1/3 yard white for rosettes and buds
* 1 yard dark pink
* 1 1/4 yards light pink
* All fabrics in the Colonial Rose quilt are made of cotton sateen, sometimes a preferred cloth for the 1930s appliquéd quilts

CUTTING DIRECTIONS:

Cut:

* 9 - 20 1/2" background squares
* 36 light pink A hearts
* 36 dark pink B hearts
* 24 white C buds
* 24 light D pink petals
* 24 dark pink E calyx
* 36 light green F calyx/leaf
* 9 white G rosettes
* 4 light green J corner swags
* 12 light green I swags
* 36 H dark pink buds for the blocks

THE BLOCKS APPEAR TO BE ON POINT; HOWEVER, IT IS THE APPLIQUE UNIT THAT IS ON POINT.

SEWING DIRECTIONS:

Choose your favorite method for appliqué and prepare the pieces.

Create flower units using templates A, B, F, G and H for each of the 9 squares. Place the appliqué units on point beginning in the center of blocks as shown.

Appliqué all blocks on point and set the 9 finished blocks together as shown on page 92.

BORDERS AND SWAGS:

Cut top and bottom borders 12 1/2" x 60 1/2".
Cut 2 side borders 12 1/2" x 84 1/2".

See figure #1. Refer to the photo of the quilt for placement of appliqués.

Place 3 swags in middle of each border and appliqué in place.

Sew the corner swags into the corners of quilt.

QUILTING:

Choose a feathered wreath for quilting spaces where the blocks meet.

Quilt in a 1/2" or 3/4" square grid, on point, around and between the flower units, trailing feathers, and around the border swags.

Colonial Rose

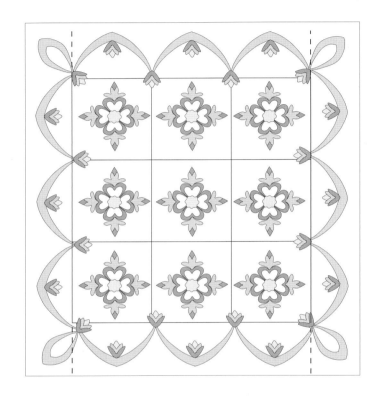

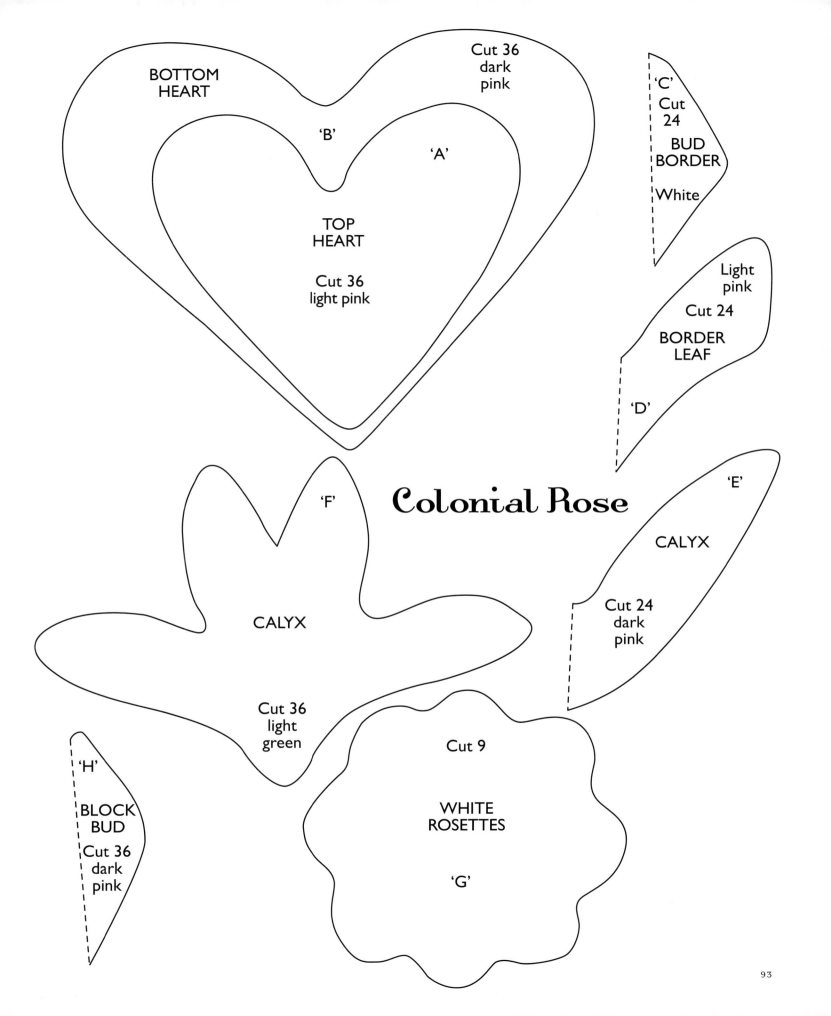

BOTTOM HEART

Cut 36 dark pink

'B'

'A'

TOP HEART

Cut 36 light pink

'C' Cut 24

BUD BORDER

White

Light pink

Cut 24

BORDER LEAF

'D'

'F'

Colonial Rose

'E'

CALYX

Cut 24 dark pink

CALYX

Cut 36 light green

Cut 9

WHITE ROSETTES

'G'

'H'

BLOCK BUD

Cut 36 dark pink

93

Colonial Rose

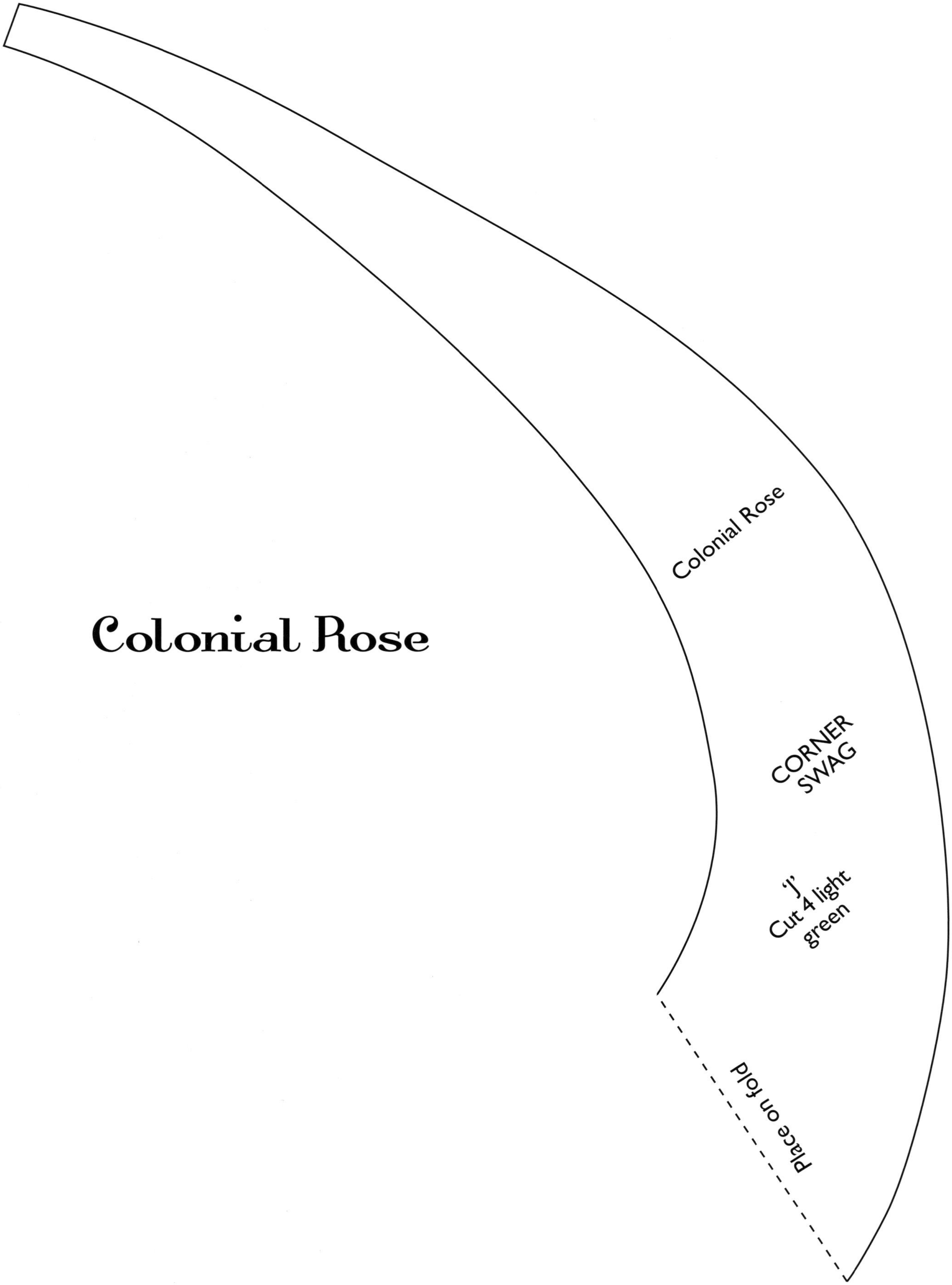

Colonial Rose

CORNER
SWAG

'J'
Cut 4 light
green

Place on fold

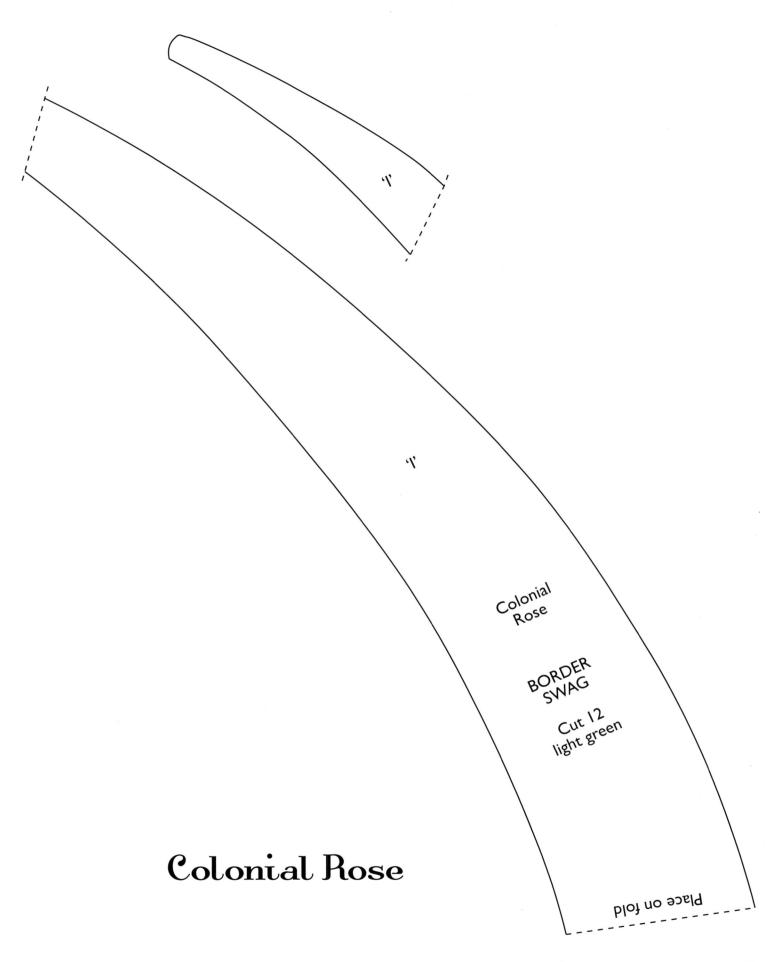

Colonial
Rose

BORDER
SWAG

Cut 12
light green

Place on fold

Colonial Rose

Through this most lonely and disheartening of all winters, I have found my greatest inspiration and encouragement in the blossoming plants in our windows...
—CAROLYN HENDERSON

You would have taken pleasure, as we did, in the fields of golden coreopsis, in the banks of salmon-colored mallow, in the mats of vivid purple verbena, in scattered plants here and there of white and lilac beard tongue, and in several varieties of evening primrose-lemon yellow, pink, and white...
—CAROLYN HENDERSON

In the spring we had our first experience with dirt storms.
The failure of crops the preceding year had left the whole country
bare and exposed to the pulverizing action of the frosts. When the
March winds began in earnest, the first flew in clouds, so that
often we could not see as far as the barn, and the dirt was almost
as thick in the house as out of doors.

I must thank you for the hyacinths and their message.
As I grow older, I realize more and more the truth
that "man cannot live by bread alone." And now even
when the matter of bread seems a problem, I am
thankful. Indeed, that other things than material
comfort do enter in to make life worthwhile after all.
—CAROLYN HENDERSON

WINDOW GARDEN

Designed and made by Terry Clothier Thompson.
The dress was made between 1930–1940 using feedsack fabric.
The embroidered apron is also from that time period.

Window Garden

SIZE: 24" X 58"

YARDAGE:

* 1 3/4 yards of plain or small print fabric, for the background of the appliquéd rose and daffodils or use feedsack fabric or reproductions prints that has the 1930s look.
* 1 fat quarter of shaded brown for bucket
* 1/4 yard brown for daffodil pot
* 3" x 11" strip of light brown for the inside of the bucket and the pot.
* 1 fat quarter of light tan for bucket handle or a scrap large enough to cut a 2" x 16" bias strip
* 1 fat quarter of shaded green for rose stem and leaves, daffodil stems and leaves
* 1 fat quarter shaded yellow and scrap of dark yellow for daffodils
* 6" x 8" piece of red and scraps of light, medium and dark pink for rose petals
* 1 yard of 30s print for curtain
* An old window that measures at least 24" x 56" or adjust your quilt to fit a window of your choice

CUTTING INSTRUCTIONS:

Cut background fabric 26" x 58" or to fit your window. I left 2" extra so the background will fill the window and can be tacked to the sides of the frame.

Refer to the templates on pages 100-105 for the cutting instructions for the appliqué pieces.

Prepare all appliqué pieces for using your favorite method.

ROSE:

Layer and appliqué rose pieces B – C – D – E – F – G and H on top of red rose piece A. Sew all in place as shown in the diagram on page 100.

Sew top of bucket K to bucket L.

For the bucket handle, cut a 2" x 16" bias strip and use a 1" bias maker to turn the edges under. Sew the handle to bucket. Refer to the placement diagram on page 102.

Pin all the elements in place. Put rose stem T behind the bucket. Pin the appliquéd rose and the leaves to the background. Appliqué all in place.

DAFFODILS:

Make the pot by sewing piece I to piece J.

Sew center P to the top of piece O. Add piece R. Arrange 5 Q petals around each P-O-R unit of the daffodil when you place the flowers.

Place the S stem and N leaves in pot.

Place the daffodil flowers between the leaves. Appliqué in place.

Hem '30s print for curtain to hang straight or in swag to the side of the window.

Gather the top and sew the curtain to the top of the appliquéd background.

Hang your window in the kitchen or sewing room.

Window Garden

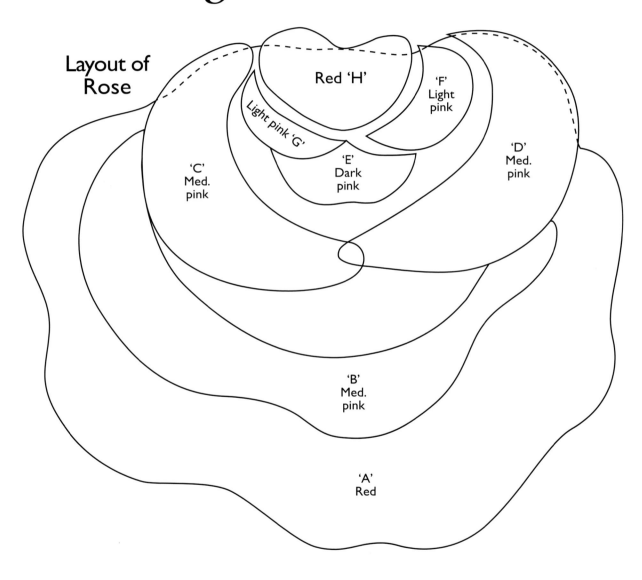

Layout of
Rose

Red 'H'

'F'
Light
pink

Light pink 'G'

'E'
Dark
pink

'D'
Med.
pink

'C'
Med.
pink

'B'
Med.
pink

'A'
Red

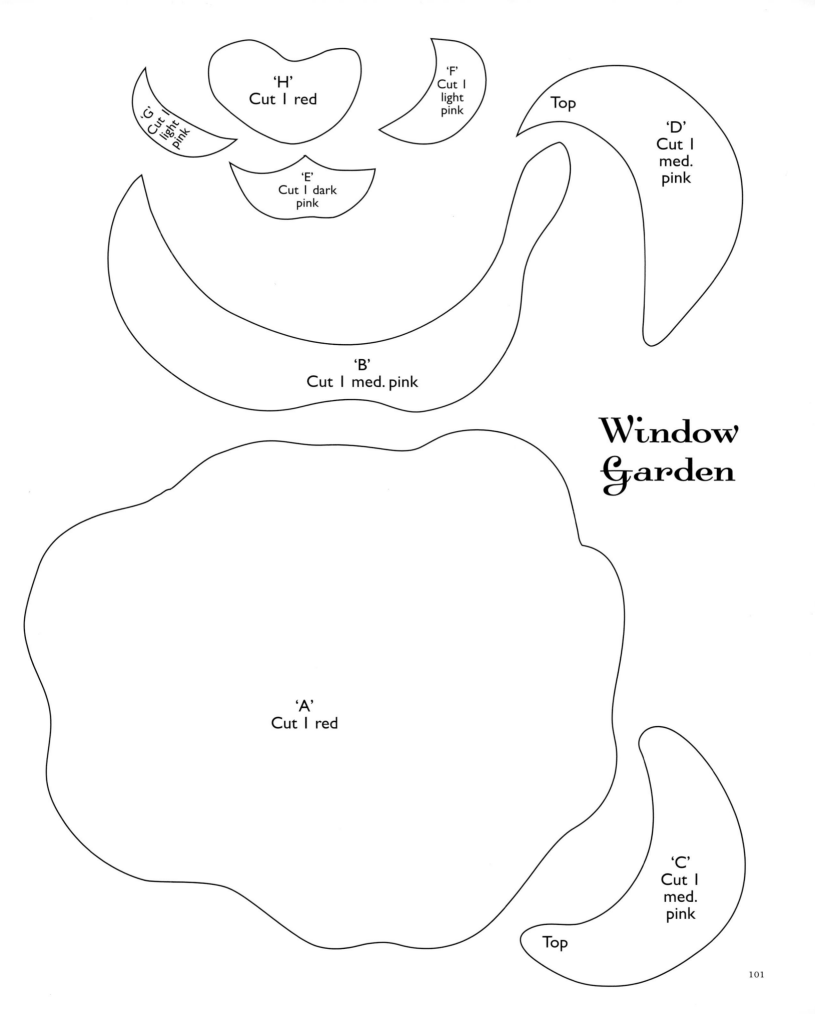

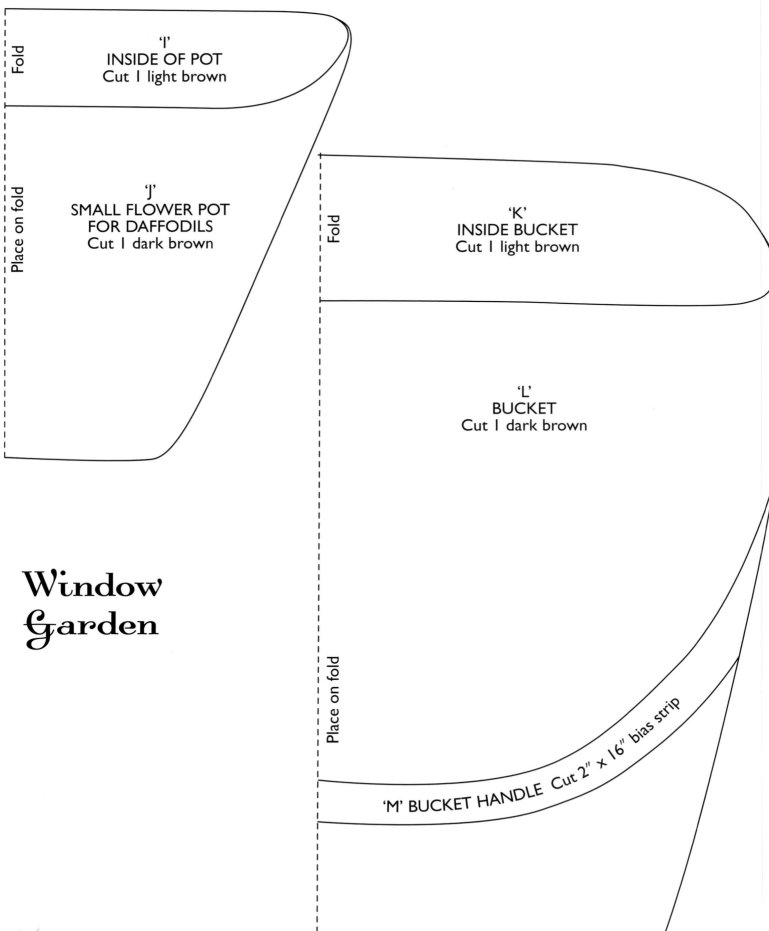

'I'
INSIDE OF POT
Cut 1 light brown

Fold

Place on fold

'J'
SMALL FLOWER POT
FOR DAFFODILS
Cut 1 dark brown

Fold

'K'
INSIDE BUCKET
Cut 1 light brown

'L'
BUCKET
Cut 1 dark brown

Place on fold

Window Garden

'M' BUCKET HANDLE Cut 2" x 16" bias strip

Daffodils

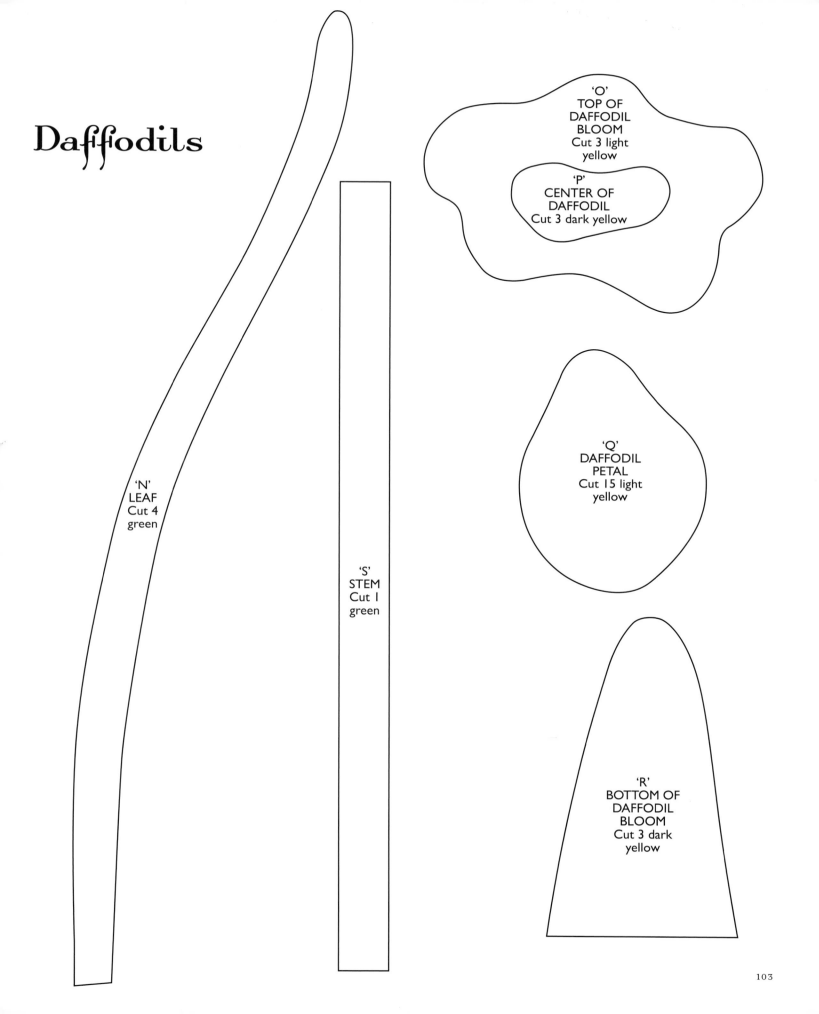

'O'
TOP OF
DAFFODIL
BLOOM
Cut 3 light
yellow

'P'
CENTER OF
DAFFODIL
Cut 3 dark yellow

'N'
LEAF
Cut 4
green

'S'
STEM
Cut 1
green

'Q'
DAFFODIL
PETAL
Cut 15 light
yellow

'R'
BOTTOM OF
DAFFODIL
BLOOM
Cut 3 dark
yellow

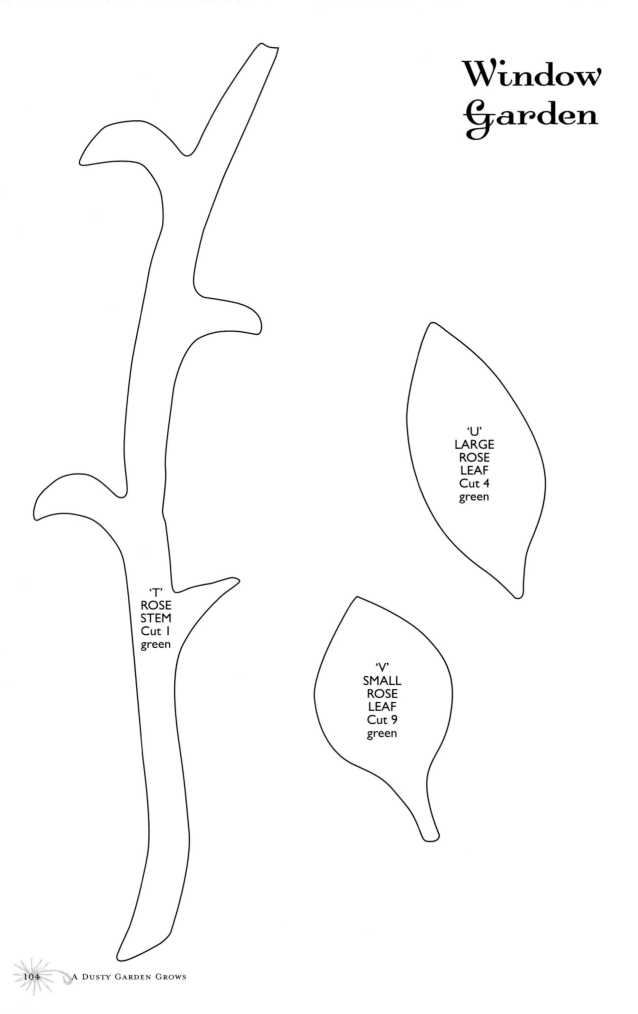

Window Garden

'U'
LARGE
ROSE
LEAF
Cut 4
green

'T'
ROSE
STEM
Cut 1
green

'V'
SMALL
ROSE
LEAF
Cut 9
green

Window Garden

SUE WALKS IN HER GARDEN
Framed pressed flower picture made by Terry Clothier Thompson: 12" x 15"

Sue Walks in Her Garden

SIZE: 12" X 15"

YARDAGE AND SUPPLIES

* 1 fat quarter light print, for background—15" x 18"
* 6" x 8" rectangle of print for Sue's dress
* 1 fat quarter of a solid fabric for her matching hat, sleeve and shoe.
* Scrap of muslin for her hand
* Embroidery floss for sun bonnet
* Roxanne's Glue Baste It.
* Poster board the size of the glass in your frame.
* Pressed flowers on stems, such as larkspur, pansies or columbine
* 12" x 15" frame with glass

Use the glass as a pattern for cutting the poster board. Place the cut poster board in the middle of the background fabric, draw around the glass with a pencil on the wrong side of the background fabric. Cut 2" away from the pencil line.

SEWING DIRECTIONS

Refer to the sewing directions in the "Sue Lives" chapter. Place Sue in the center of the background fabric and appliqué in place.

Place the dried stems and flowers around Sue as shown in the photo. Use just a drop of glue to hold them in place.

Center the cut poster board on the pencil guide lines and put the background right side down.
Glue and turn the outer edges of the background to the poster board.

When your picture is complete, put the glass over the picture and carefully place it inside the frame. Check for and remove any falling debris.

Secure the picture with small framing nails or the staples that came with the frame.

Bibliography

1. *The Next Greatest Thing- 50 years of Rural Electrification in America.* 1984, NRECA.

2. *Beneath the Window.* Patricia Wilson Clothier, Early Ranch Life in the Big Bend Country- Iron Mountain Press 2003

3. *Letters from the Dust Bowl-*Caroline Henderson. University of Oklahoma Press

4. *Diary* – based on Terry's family stories and recollections-Written by Terry Clothier Thompson. 1993